Praise for *The Way to*

The Way to Inclusion provides a powerful intersection of values-driven leadership, visioning for equity, strategic support and learning, data-driven decision making, and, most important, understanding and believing in the *strengths and possibilities* of both your staff and your students. Leaders now have a roadmap to assist them in providing a welcoming, rigorous, and compassionate school for all learners.

Heather Greicius, Executive Director of Special Populations,
Adams 12 Five Star Schools, Colorado

The Way to Inclusion is essential for district and school building leaders as they engage in the complexities of systems change. The pages should be read, highlighted, dog-eared, and riddled with handwritten comments in the margins as leaders roll up their sleeves and get to work applying what is written to change hearts and minds and create equitable, inclusive systems of education for each and every student.

Jennifer Sommerness, EdS, TIES Center, University of Minnesota

The Way to Inclusion provides a practical, adaptable, and inclusive approach to creating more inclusive schools and systems and promotes and embraces an abundance of strategies and resources that can be used to fit any educational setting, no matter its size, culture and climate, or other perceived barriers. The Inclusive System Change Path presented in this book, with accompanying recommendations and real-life examples of implementation, is a top-tier resource contributing to the urgent work that must be done toward supporting inclusive education. *The Way to Inclusion* is a must-read for anyone learning about, leading, or participating in systems change toward highly inclusive and effective schools.

Jaylee Swanson, Director of Special Education,
East Moline School District, Illinois

This is a book that every leader should read. Inclusive education focuses on transforming the system to include every student in the learning community where all learners grow and thrive. Special education is not a place, but a system of supports wrapped around students where every school staff member has a role. *The Way to Inclusion* offers leaders a path to success with powerful strategies to develop vision, reimagine school structures, and promote effective collaboration among educators.

Marcia Blum, Preschool Special Education Specialist,
Exceptional Student Services, Colorado Department of Education

The Way to Inclusion is a much-needed call to action. But more than that, this engaging, accessible book provides a path to progress—a systematic, practical approach to help educators build inclusive schools, overcome obstacles, and reach the results that the law, research, and conscience demand for *all* learners. A wonderful gift for anyone committed to or curious about achieving better outcomes and creating truly inclusive learning communities.

Patrick G. Radel, Esq., attorney, advocate, and parent

The authors of *The Way to Inclusion* have developed a comprehensive and practical guide for leadership teams working toward systems-level inclusive change. This book provides research to address the *why* of inclusion alongside steps and strategies that explain *how*.

Danielle Nahorney, Director of Academic Services and Accountability, Baldwinsville Central School District, New York

If you are an educational leader looking to deliver a more inclusive education to students while supporting staff in this work, this is the book for you. *The Way to Inclusion* includes advice from those who were the "boots on the ground" and made meaningful progress in educating all children in integrated settings. This book provides the knowledge and tools needed to develop and implement an inclusive plan while giving guidance to avoid common missteps. It's a must-read roadmap for current and future educators, leaders, and change makers.

Dr. Joyce A. Carr, Supervisor of Special Education, upstate New York

This is a brilliant tool for all school leaders who want to improve service delivery for *all* students who have been historically marginalized in our schools while simultaneously meeting the standard of IDEA. The authors have constructed a roadmap with milestones to guide schools and districts toward providing a liberated education for all of their stakeholders.

Deborah Hoffman, PhD, Associate Superintendent, Madison Metropolitan School District, Wisconsin

the way to inclusion

Also by Julie Causton and Kate MacLeod

Building a Positive and Supportive Classroom (Quick Reference Guide)

From Behaving to Belonging: The Inclusive Art of Supporting Students Who Challenge Us

julie **CAUSTON** / *kate* **MACLEOD**
kristie **PRETTI-FRONTCZAK**
jenna mancini **RUFO** / *paul* **GORDON**

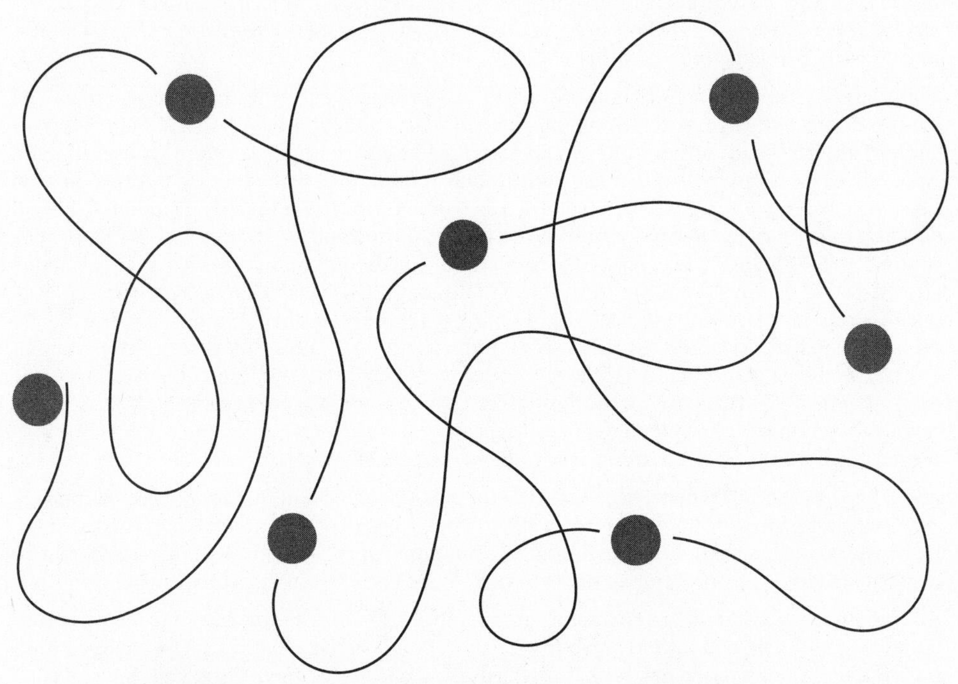

the way to inclusion

How Leaders Create Schools Where Every Student Belongs

Arlington, Virginia USA

2800 Shirlington Road, Suite 1001 • Arlington, VA 22206 USA
Phone: 800-933-2723 or 703-578-9600 • Fax: 703-575-5400
Website: www.ascd.org • Email: member@ascd.org
Author guidelines: www.ascd.org/write

Penny Reinart, *Deputy Executive Director*; Genny Ostertag, *Managing Director, Book Acquisitions & Editing;* Stephanie Bize, *Acquisitions Editor;* Mary Beth Nielsen, *Director, Book Editing;* Miriam Calderone, *Editor;* Thomas Lytle, *Creative Director;* Donald Ely, *Art Director;* Valerie Younkin, *Senior Production Designer;* Kelly Marshall, *Production Manager;* Shajuan Martin, *E-Publishing Specialist*

PAPERBACK ISBN: 978-1-4166-3180-4 ASCD product #123001 n5/23

PDF EBOOK ISBN: 978-1-4166-3181-1; see Books in Print for other formats.

Quantity discounts are available: email programteam@ascd.org or call 800-933-2723, ext. 5773, or 703-575-5773. For desk copies, go to www.ascd.org/deskcopy.

Library of Congress Cataloging-in-Publication Data
Names: Causton, Julie, author.
Title: The way to inclusion : how leaders create schools where every student belongs / Julie Causton, Kate MacLeod, Kristie Pretti-Frontczak, Jenna Mancini Rufo, Paul Gordon.
Description: Arlington, VA : ASCD, 2023. | Includes bibliographical references and index.
Identifiers: LCCN 2022053721 (print) | LCCN 2022053722 (ebook) | ISBN 9781416631804 (paperback) | ISBN 9781416631811 (pdf)
Subjects: LCSH: Inclusive education. | Mainstreaming in education. | Educational equalization. | School environment. | Classroom environment.
Classification: LCC LC1201 .C376 2023 (print) | LCC LC1201 (ebook) | DDC 371.9/046–dc23/eng/20230103
LC record available at https://lccn.loc.gov/2022053721
LC ebook record available at https://lccn.loc.gov/2022053722

32 31 30 29 28 27 26 25 24 2 3 4 5 6 7 8 9 10 11 12

the way to inclusion

How Leaders Create Schools Where Every Student Belongs

Acknowledgments

Julie—To everyone on the path!

Kate—Thank you to all the fabulous colleagues, leaders, educators, families, and legal advocates I've worked with and learned from over the years!

Kristie—With gratitude to all my teachers and coaches who instilled in me a passion for getting to the core of systemic inequities, while keeping a focus on hope and possibilities.

Jenna—Many thanks to my husband Patrick and amazing children, Eva and Emma, as well as to the mentors in my life who helped me become the leader I am today!

Paul—I would like to thank my incredible wife, Marianne, for always being my number one champion, for, without her, none of my work would be possible. I would also like to recognize the amazingly talented team members I have worked with over the last 25 years in education, especially Heather, Lauren, and Trisha!

Introduction

Welcome! We are thrilled you are here seeking a way to create an inclusive school system. You likely picked up this book because you are committed to ensuring more inclusive educational experiences for all your students. Hopefully, you have come seeking strategies and inspiration to expand the mindsets, heartsets, and skillsets of the incredible educators in your system. *The Way to Inclusion* is based on the knowledge that, through bold leadership and courageous perseverance, true inclusive change can and will occur in our schools.

Our aim as the authors of this book is to walk with you from where you are now to where you desire to go on your inclusivity journey. We wish to support you every step of the way and will use our collective knowledge, our extensive experience, and a set of milestone questions to guide you. We will also provide leadership tools, reflective questions, and action steps, and highlight the skills you need to develop the inclusive school system that you desire and that your students deserve.

Your Guides

We would like to begin by introducing ourselves and sharing the experiences and philosophies that underpin every aspect of the book. These are not the polished bios you may be used to, but unvarnished versions of our truths, since we are going to ask you to be deeply honest with us, too. We find that it is impossible to separate our personal experiences from the professional work of creating inclusive systems. We believe that the confluence of our values, beliefs, and experiences influences all the ideas and strategies we share.

Again, welcome! We are glad to be on this journey with you. Here's a little bit from each of us on who we are and what we bring to the journey.

Julie Causton

Hailing from the Land of 10,000 Lakes, I am the mother of two beautiful kids. I see possibilities everywhere. I have worked in elementary, middle, and high school as a special education teacher. Because I have always believed deeply in inclusive education, I have always taught in inclusive settings—even if I had to design those settings first. I attended the University of Wisconsin–Madison, where I learned from education superstars about the inequity inherent in traditional special education programs and became singularly focused on changing those systems.

In my first position as a special educator, when the principal handed me a key to my special education classroom, I boldly handed it back. "You can turn that room into something else," I said, convinced that these students were going to be in general education classrooms. However, I quickly realized that I was in no position as a new educator to make any lasting schoolwide changes. I loved the work and the students, but I struggled to handle the backlash to the changes I sought.

I continued to teach as I went on to get my master's and doctorate degrees in inclusive education. Then I spent 14 years at Syracuse University as a tenured professor, teaching future educators how to create inclusive schools and classrooms. I had several research projects in primary and secondary schools, where I studied the change process and focused on how to create more equitable and inclusive classrooms. I have also coauthored eight best-selling books on the topic of inclusion and more than 40 peer-reviewed articles.

Over the past 25 years, inclusive education has been my life. I strive to make our education system more inclusive and equitable for all. I started a company, Inclusive Schooling, to provide educators with transformative professional development. I deeply love supporting the education leaders and teachers who are courageous enough to improve our society through inclusion.

Kate MacLeod

I am a new mother, and despite months of sleep deprivation, I was quick to say "heck yes" to coauthoring a supportive guidebook for leaders committed to the work of inclusion. I have worked in the field of education for two decades. Providing all students meaningful access to education and a sense of belonging in schools has been at the forefront of my thinking, my teaching, my research, and my writing.

I got my start in education as a public high school special educator in New York City supporting students with the most complex needs—incredible students who deserved much more than what the current system was providing. I worked with colleagues and families to rethink segregated education for students with learning difficulties, striving to include them as much as possible alongside their general education peers and within their communities.

My high school students inspired me to enter academia to support inclusive change in our education system at large. I've served on the faculty of higher education institutions in New York City and rural Maine and have also worked as an educational consultant, helping administrators and teachers throughout the country engage in the invigorating work of inclusive reform.

Throughout my career, I have been on the emotional and intellectual roller-coaster of inclusive school change, whether that's meant navigating emotionally charged meetings with families on the benefits of inclusive education or problem solving with teachers and administrators through new place-based challenges. I have also learned to connect with mentors and allies to navigate challenges and celebrate successes. With this community of support, I feel more prepared to help leaders roll up their sleeves and commit to inclusive change.

I am so glad you've joined us here so we can help *you* create inclusive change in your own school system.

Kristie Pretti-Frontczak

I love the full continuum of learners, from the youngest and newest to the oldest and most experienced. I began my career in early education curious about how young children grow and develop and was excited to discover what was possible when kind, creative educators saw the strengths and gifts of all children—especially those with significant support needs. I was an early interventionist.

Despite my curiosity and the endless possibilities of my first few years in the profession, I soon found early childhood educators to be among the most devalued and isolated people in the school system. Too often, they receive the least funding, training, and respect while still being expected to do one of the hardest jobs there is: providing quality child-centered education during the most critical period of development. These educators are also expected to do this vital work for less pay, in partnership with a whole variety of agencies, and in collaboration with a range of beautifully diverse families. I have also found that many early educators are the only voices within the system advocating for more inclusive services. Before long, I became passionate about helping to dismantle segregated early childhood programs and creating inclusive ones.

I still love everything about early childhood inclusion, but these days I focus on the other end of the continuum, helping adult learners to maintain their passion and ensure system-level changes that benefit children and their families. I first started focusing on adult learners during my 16 years as a tenured professor at Kent State University, where I taught future educators, directed grants, mentored hundreds of graduate students, and authored many articles, chapters, and books related to supporting young children in inclusive settings.

Since 2013, I have followed my true passion for designing and delivering transformative professional development as an entrepreneur. I currently partner with my coauthor Julie at Inclusive Schooling to create schools where all students flourish and educational systems, practices, and spaces are reimagined. I love teaching leaders how to raise their emotional intelligence to create kinder, more inclusive, and more creative schools for all.

To date, I have accumulated more than 50,000 hours helping educators and leaders work from a place of compassion, hope, and love everywhere from Cincinnati to Singapore. I spend just about every waking minute finding ways to support educational leaders as they engage in equity-based systems change and ensure inclusive education for our youngest citizens. I am thrilled to bring my experiences to this book as we aim to support you on this critical journey.

Jenna Mancini Rufo

I always knew I would be a special education teacher, thanks to the profound experience of growing up with a sibling with a disability. Living with my sister, Nina, who has multiple severe impairments, sparked my passion for special education. Nina attended a separate school and never had the opportunity to access grade-level curriculum and peers.

As a child, I certainly didn't have much experience with the idea of inclusion. Sure, I wished Nina could go to school with me, but I had no idea what that would look like. Even after getting a degree in elementary and special education, I still didn't get it. It was only when I was completing my master's in educational administration at Harvard University that I realized inclusive special education service delivery was far superior to anything I had previously seen.

Shortly after my master's program, I accepted a role as an inclusion facilitator at a public middle school in Massachusetts coordinating services for general education students with significant disabilities. I was privileged to be part of a system that, 20 years ago, had already been implementing inclusion for a long time.

When I moved back to my home state of Pennsylvania, however, I was shocked. Most districts there still relied on segregated and self-contained special education programming. I felt like I had stepped back in time. I decided to pursue administrative positions, confident that I could share what I knew about inclusion to benefit students.

In North Penn, a large public school district, I served as a special education supervisor and director and as assistant superintendent. In these roles, I transitioned the district from a system of self-contained special education to a more inclusive model. It was not easy. Through blood, sweat, and tears—well, maybe not blood, but definitely sweat and tears—students with disabilities became part of the fabric of the district's general education classrooms. I can say without a doubt that it was the most challenging aspect of my career in education, and with equal certainty that it was the most rewarding.

Today, I take my knowledge as a school leader around the country to help schools implement inclusion as the founder of empowerED School Solutions. I am excited to have this opportunity to share my insights with you alongside my amazing coauthors, Julie, Paul, Kate, and Kristie!

Paul Gordon

I love being an educator. Seeing the impact that educators have on students' lives fills me with the energy, focus, and drive I need to do better for each student. My journey to cowriting this book was a long one that taught me about the abilities of our students and the power educators have to transform their lives.

I believe that inclusive schooling is one of the most complex system changes in education. Yet unlike my amazing coauthors, I don't have an academic background in special education. What I bring to the table are my experiences as an educator.

I reflect on my time working at a middle school in Colorado with students like Vinny and JT, who were assigned to my reading class because they were reading two to five years below grade level but did not receive special education services. These brilliant young students had to attend my class while their friends took elective courses like P.E., art, technology, or music. They hated walking into my room because they were segregated from their peers, which made them feel like they didn't belong.

I think about my colleagues when I was a principal in Colorado in the early 2000s and began to think differently about segregating students in "reading," "resource," or "self-contained" classrooms. Educators like Jenny, Teresa, Tina, Stacy, Lisa, Jess, and others asked the question, "Why do some kids get access to general education classes and diverse peers while others are hidden away in small classrooms where no one sees them?" We began to think about where our students would learn best and how we could support each student's learning. Was it perfect? Nope. But we did not allow the idea of perfection to get in the way of doing better for our students.

I think about my time as the chief academic officer for a large school district in Colorado, where we developed a multitiered system of support, took a new approach to instruction and assessment, and started knocking down the silos that divide our district. We thought about our work from a systems perspective rather than an individual school perspective.

I reflect on my time as superintendent in the western suburbs of Chicago, where some students with IEPs were sent to other school districts to receive their education. We moved students out of resource rooms and allowed them to access the general education setting. Was it incredibly challenging? Absolutely. Did we do better by our students? Absolutely. These opportunities in education are what led me to cowrite this book. I am proud to be a coauthor alongside my incredible fellow educators.

Preparing for Your Journey

You have decided to embark on an important and courageous journey to create a more inclusive school system. Such a journey requires planning and preparation. In *The Way to Inclusion,* we offer practical tools and concrete strategies that can be adopted immediately, including an Inclusive System Change Path, action planning templates, and timelines. We share examples and personal stories from our experiences and the experiences of other educational leaders to illustrate the successes and challenges of implementing inclusive educational change. In each chapter, we guide you through key ideas, structures, and practices that you will use to implement inclusive change. We point out obstacles you may encounter and offer supportive guidance to help you find your way.

What Is Inclusion?

But what exactly *is* inclusion? This term often means different things to different people. As your guides, we are here to help you and your staff clarify the answer to this question. You must have a clear and deep understanding of inclusion to lead real, sustainable systems change.

Our definition of inclusion disrupts the inequities found in traditional special education systems. It is a bold and courageous call to those committed to creating schools where students thrive together. This definition is at the heart of the inclusive change process used throughout this book.

> We no longer accept that separate classrooms, separate schools, and separate lives are in the best interest of any student. Separating people by ability disadvantages everyone. Belonging is a human need. Our educational system, practices, and spaces need to be reimagined.
>
> Every student is valued because of their strengths, gifts, and even challenges. As disability is simply diversity. Everyone benefits from meaningful participation and opportunities to learn grade-level content with diverse peers. We must trust that all students come to us as incredible, whole people who do not need to be fixed (Causton & Pretti-Frontczak, 2021a).

We define inclusion as multidimensional because it involves all aspects of the school system. Inclusion means students who have any type of educational label are educated together and teachers collaborate and co-teach to design lessons for all. It involves creating welcoming spaces where students' multiple identities are seen and celebrated, and continually and seamlessly providing students with access to additional support. Inclusive practices require partnering with families in new ways, understanding our own biases, and bravely examining where the system currently fails our students.

The Inclusive System Change Path

We've organized this book around the Inclusive System Change Path (Causton, MacLeod, & Pretti-Frontczak, 2022a), a framework grounded in the in-depth inclusive system reform process that we have used throughout the United

States for more than 25 years, findings from nearly 50 years of research on what makes inclusion work, and our own experiences creating inclusive schools. We turned this extensive knowledge into the Inclusive System Change Path, which contains milestones, clarifying questions, and leadership steps that will help to guide real change and inclusive growth in your school system (see Figure I.1).

Each chapter in this book aligns with a milestone question from the Inclusive System Change Path. The questions are meant to help you identify and understand your system's current strengths and needs, guiding your pursuit of meaningful inclusive change. Though the order of the milestone questions is sequential, we know that individual systems change is not linear. We have used this framework in many different systems—large, small, rural, urban, and suburban—and understand that each system's unique context will create many opportunities for shortcuts and necessary redirects, circle-backs, and loops. The icon below, preceding Figure I.1, provides a visual of this path, complete with milestones and loops.

This journey can take anywhere from three to five years to complete. Great leaders will keep the urgency of the work at the center while going at a pace their system can tolerate, all the while supporting their colleagues with clarity, compassion, and purpose. Leading systems change will be among the most challenging but also rewarding and impactful work you are likely to complete in your educational career. We are here to support you all along the way.

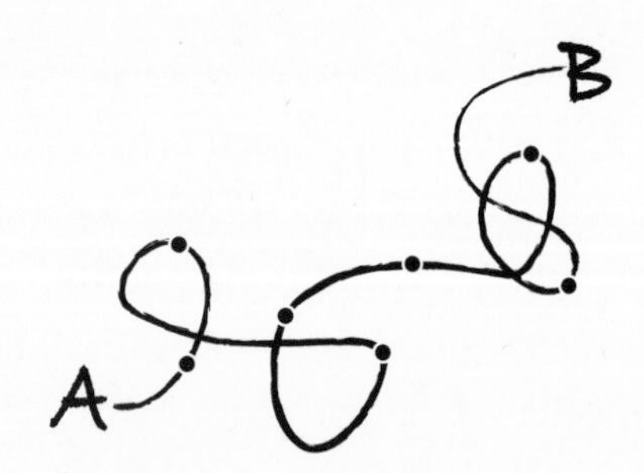

Figure I.1 Inclusive System Change Path

Milestone 1: Do we understand why inclusive education is the way forward?

Leadership Questions
Q 1.1 Is the leadership team clear on what inclusion means?
Q 1.2 Do we understand the equity lens?
Q 1.3 How will the leadership team explore their own "why"?
Q 1.4 Does the leadership team know how to communicate why inclusion is the way forward?

Leadership Steps
S 1.1 Develop a shared understanding of inclusive education.
S 1.2 Explore the equity lens together.
S 1.3 Read and discuss the reasons why people engage in this work.
S 1.4 As a team, explore your personal "whys."
S 1.5 Support leaders who continue to have questions about inclusion.

Milestone 2: Have we seen our system through an equity lens?

Leadership Questions
Q 2.1 Which students are not educated within their home school or home school district?
Q 2.2 Which students do not have access to general education classrooms, content, and peers for most of the day?
Q 2.3 Which students are over- or underrepresented in special education, in more restrictive placements, or in terms of disciplinary action?
Q 2.4 Which students are still in separate programs or classrooms for students with specific disabilities?
Q 2.5 Do educators and related service providers work in collaborative teams?
Q 2.6 Do any special educators or related service providers work in separate rooms, spaces, or programs?

Leadership Steps
S 2.1 Collect system data using the Equity Review Data Collection Guide.
S 2.2 Visually represent system equity data using graphs or charts.
S 2.3 Create building-level service-delivery maps.
S 2.4 Share the system data with the leadership team and analyze it through an equity lens.
S 2.5 Name and take action to remedy inequities in the current system.

Milestone 3: Do we have a clear public vision for inclusion and understanding of the needed system-level changes?

Leadership Questions
Q 3.1 Does the leadership team have a vision for inclusion?
Q 3.2 Does the leadership team have a clear rationale for the shift toward inclusion?
Q 3.3 Has the leadership team included diverse members in the visioning process?
Q 3.4 Is the vision shared publicly?
Q 3.5 Is there a process in place to revisit and revise the vision yearly?

Leadership Steps
S 3.1 Craft or revise a vision statement.
S 3.2 Develop a clear rationale using key findings from your system equity review.
S 3.3 Get feedback on the vision from diverse members of the school system.
S 3.4 Share the finalized vision and rationale widely.
S 3.5 Review the vision and rationale yearly, revising as needed.

Milestone 4: How can we realign existing service-delivery structures to create an inclusive system?

Leadership Questions
Q 4.1 Where are our service-delivery structures out of alignment with our inclusive vision?
Q 4.2 How do we better align service-delivery structures to our inclusive vision?
Q 4.3 How do we use the IEP as a vehicle for effective inclusive change?

(continued)

Figure I.1 Inclusive System Change Path—(*continued*)

Milestone 4: How can we realign existing service-delivery structures to create an inclusive system?—(*continued*)
Leadership Steps **S 4.1** Review service-delivery maps before and after inclusive redesign. **S 4.2** Use system data to align service-delivery structures with your inclusive vision. **S 4.3** Align IEPs with new inclusive structures.
Milestone 5: How can we reimagine schedules and collaborative staff roles?
Leadership Questions **Q 5.1** How can the leadership team strategically and flexibly schedule existing staff? **Q 5.2** How will the leadership team explore and communicate the reimagined collaborative roles and responsibilities for new inclusive service delivery? **Q 5.3** How will the leadership team ensure and support collaborative instructional planning time? **Leadership Steps** **S 5.1** Learn about collaborative roles and inclusive service delivery. **S 5.2** Identify ways to strategically and flexibly schedule staff to serve all students inclusively. **S 5.3** Carve out time in the schedule for staff to collaboratively plan and provide ongoing support.
Milestone 6: Do our educators use powerful inclusive classroom practices?
Leadership Questions **Q 6.1** Does the leadership team understand the most powerful inclusive classroom practices? **Q 6.2** Does the leadership team have a highly effective professional development plan to address collaboration and co-teaching, differentiation, adaptations, and natural and behavioral supports? **Q 6.3** Does the leadership team provide staff with effective learning opportunities to support implementation of powerful inclusive classroom practices? **Q 6.4** Does the leadership team provide staff with feedback on powerful inclusive classroom practices to ensure accountability and meaningful support? **Leadership Steps** **S 6.1** Explore highly effective inclusive classroom practices and identify growth opportunities. **S 6.2** Develop a systematic plan for all-staff professional development about powerful inclusive classroom practices. **S 6.3** Create learning that gives staff opportunities to learn with one another and from student advocates and inclusion experts. **S 6.4** Communicate expectations to staff and provide feedback on those expectations.
Milestone 7: How can we provide ongoing support for this new inclusive system?
Leadership Questions **Q 7.1** Does the leadership team understand systems change? **Q 7.2** Does the leadership team understand how to support everyone through change? **Q 7.3** Does the leadership team have a systematic way to analyze educators' successes and needs? **Q 7.4** Does the leadership team have a way to sustain the momentum of change? **Q 7.5** Does the leadership team document progress and celebrate often? **Leadership Steps** **S 7.1** Explore systems change. **S 7.2** Learn more about how to support everyone through change. **S 7.3** Design a systematic way to analyze educators' successes and needs. **S 7.4** Determine ways to sustain the momentum of change. **S 7.5** Create genuine systems of celebration.

Source: Causton, J., MacLeod, K., & Pretti-Frontczak, K. (2022a). *The Inclusive System Change Path*. New York: Inclusive Schooling, LLC.

What Else Is in the Book?

Each chapter in this book aligns with a broad milestone question, a series of clarifying questions, and leadership steps. At the beginning of each chapter, we ask you to consider the broad milestone question. We then walk you through each of the leadership steps—the main part of each chapter—and conclude by asking you to review and discuss the questions and steps with your leadership team. Finally, we ask you to determine your system's specific next steps and write them in your Action Plan. We have provided you with a template that you can use for this purpose (available in Appendix A, p. 113, and at www.inclusiveschooling.com/the-way-to-inclusion or www.ascd.org/the-way-to-inclusion-resources).

The path to inclusion is both strenuous and inspiring. We recommend that you work your way through this book chapter by chapter, with your trusted leadership team by your side. Together you will make courageous decisions about the specific actions and timelines that will move your system toward greater inclusive experiences for all students. Write each action step out explicitly, including how that step will be measured, the person responsible for carrying out the action assigned, and a specific timeline for completion.

Your Action Plan will depend on your team, your leadership style, and your preferences. One efficient strategy is to set a monthly meeting to determine actions for your team. At the next meeting, the team reviews the progress and sets new action steps. The team repeats this iterative process each month until the action steps are complete, always understanding that the journey never truly ends—there will always be new challenges to address and new ways to improve equity. Another approach is to use the Action Plan to set a year's worth of goals and return to the document each quarter, again using an iterative process to complete your action steps.

Get your customizable Action Plan as well as other resources we include in this book at www.inclusiveschooling.com/the-way-to-inclusion or www.ascd.org/the-way-to-inclusion-resources.

Additional Visuals to Support Your Journey

The following three images will appear throughout the book to remind you that you are not alone and help guide you forward:

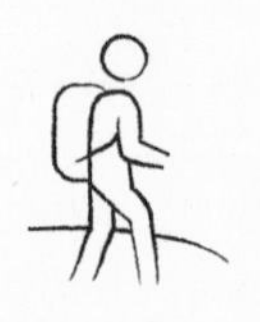

Seasoned Traveler—This image of a traveler on a path is designed to connect you to someone who has taken this journey ahead of you and can provide clear answers about how they made it through a particular challenge. Wherever this image appears, we share specific examples of how other leaders have navigated an obstacle or developed an innovative approach to inclusive change. The traveler image is a reminder that someone has come before you; it is here to support you, advise you, and let you know that you can make it through your own inclusive journey.

The Loop—This image is designed to remind you that your path will not always be linear. Throughout your journey, you may need to circle back to different sections of the book for support, or ahead for more information about a concept. Either way, use the loop to help you gain clarity and understanding.

Your Action Plan—This image prompts you to stop and add steps to your Action Plan. We have included it at the end of each chapter because we want you to translate the concepts from each chapter into actionable items that will support your system's inclusive journey. We provide specific leadership questions and steps to help you determine where your system and leadership team need to focus. Together, you and your team will use our leadership questions and steps to determine the best actions for your unique system.

You are now ready to lead the way to inclusion.

Your First Action Plan

- Decide on your leadership team—the people you want to bring to the table to do this work with you. Remember, you can always add additional members to the team as you move forward.
- Schedule a meeting to sit together and work through the beginning of this book.
- Read the definition of *inclusion* on page 7. Talk about where you are headed.
- Read about the Inclusive System Change Path on page 7 and discuss the journey ahead.
- Get your Action Plan. Use our digital template or create your own plan that clearly outlines each action item, who is responsible for the action, how you will measure success, and a deadline for completion.

1

Understand Why Inclusive Education Is the Way Forward

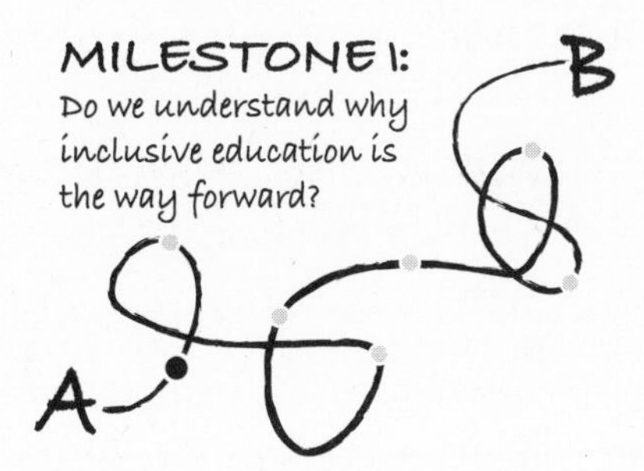

Congratulations on starting your journey! Our first milestone question is, "Do we understand why inclusive education is the way forward?" Here we set the stage for understanding why leaders like you commit to inclusive education. We explore the concept of an equity lens and share how you can clearly comprehend and communicate a rationale for inclusion to the entire school or system. In this chapter, you also can explore your "personal why" and learn ways to support your leadership team so you can all be headed in the same direction together. At the end of the chapter, we ask you to review and discuss the leadership questions and steps and determine areas that may need more attention. For reader ease, we have numbered sections of the chapter with the corresponding milestone leadership steps. Finally, we ask you to visit your Action Plan to put your steps in place.

Gain clarity on what inclusion means. Before you begin to explore your own reasons for moving to a more inclusive system, you may want to loop back and read our definition of inclusion on page 7. Some leaders use our definition as their goal, while others use it as a conversation-starter with their leadership team.

1.1: Develop a Shared Understanding of Inclusive Education

School system leaders will often disagree on the importance of inclusion. We have seen inclusive system change stall because of this. All administrators on your team must be a part of the meaning-making around inclusion—from central office staff to building leaders. To build a shared understanding, start by gathering your leadership team and thinking deeply about the change you want to see in your system. As you do so, envision how becoming more inclusive can impact the entire system. Ask team members to independently answer the following questions:

- What does inclusion mean to me? Be as detailed as possible.
- What changes in current practices will inclusion have for our school system and everyone in it?
- Think ahead one year, or even five years. What does a more inclusive system look and feel like?

Once everyone has completed their reflections, spend time discussing the similarities and differences in team members' responses. Using this time to create a shared understanding will bring clarity to the words we use, our hopes for our students, and the work that lies ahead. We encourage the team to take time with this process. Trust and honesty will be key.

Our Meaning-Making Experience

By a school superintendent

As a district and school leadership team, we began our meaning-making process by each completing an anonymous survey. This was to ensure that each of our leaders felt safe sharing their thoughts and ideas without fear of judgment. The survey asked each team member to define *inclusion* in their own words and to describe in detail what they thought inclusion would look like for students and staff when fully implemented. It also asked precisely where the wide range of diverse learners would be educated.

We started by reading aloud each definition and ideal vision for inclusion, stopping to celebrate the honesty our team put forth. This initial review revealed that we had very little shared meaning of the term *inclusion* and almost no agreement on what the ideal future state of inclusion would look like in our district. However, we celebrated even this—the fact that we *didn't* have a clear or shared understanding of inclusion or what it would look like.

Why? Because the meaning-making process worked. It was clear that our team needed more time to think, read, process, and discuss inclusion. Then, over the next six weeks, we took time for more deliberate meaning-making, during which we created a shared understanding of inclusion and our vision for what it would look like for students and staff.

1.2: Explore the Equity Lens Together

Separate special education programs, schools, and classrooms have existed for decades. For the most part, educators and parents have embraced the myth that these separate settings are beneficial despite research and lived experiences indicating otherwise. Thus, one of the greatest challenges to creating inclusive school systems is shifting mindsets away from long-held beliefs that students with disabilities benefit from separate settings to receive individualized instruction.

Leaders must address this underlying systemic message about disability grounded in an outdated and exclusionary medical model by shifting the lens through which they view disabilities. A lens provides us a way to look at something, and across many school systems today, we are using a very outdated lens to view students with disabilities—one that has been distorting our vision for some time. We suggest replacing the current lens with an equity lens to improve our vision of how we "see" or understand disability, as seen in Figure 1.1 (Causton & Pretti-Frontczak, 2021b). By changing our lens, we can create a new mindset that will eventually impact how we teach and support our learners with and without labels.

Figure 1.1 Medical Versus Equity Lens

Medical Lens	Equity Lens
• Disability is seen as residing within the individual. • Focus is on individual pathology or impairment. • Aim is to fix or remediate. • Disability labels are seen as deficits. • Labels, rather than systems, are seen as the problem. • Systemic inequities are ignored.	• Disability is seen as a socially constructed identity. • Focus is on societal barriers that disable people. • Aim is to provide "just right" supports. • Disability is seen as a natural difference. • Systems, rather than the disabilities themselves, are seen as the problem. • Systemic inequities are identified and addressed.

Source: From *The Transition from Medical to Equity Lens* by J. Causton & K. Pretti-Frontczak, 2021, Inclusive Schooling. Copyright 2021 by Inclusive Schooling. Reprinted with permission.

The Medical Lens

Today, too many schools continue to view disability through a medical lens that views it as a problem that needs to be fixed. You can hear echoes of the medical lens in our everyday special education terminology: words like *deficit, pathology, remediate,* and *therapy,* which all stem from a medical perspective. Places like resource rooms and separate classrooms for students with specific labels (autism, behavior disorder, visual impairment) were born out of these beliefs. The medical lens sees a student's disability as the problem that a specialist in a separate room is required to fix.

The Equity Lens

The equity lens provides us with a new understanding of the way systems we have created are disabling students. This lens helps us to see that disability is a form of difference or diversity, and that our job is not to fix it in a separate environment, but to help students access, participate in, and make progress in the general education setting. The equity lens allows us to see that it is systemic inequities, not our students, that need to be fixed.

Services over Placements or Programs

Special education should be considered a service rather than a separate placement or program. Rather than being seen as the purview of special education staff in special schools, self-contained programs, or resource rooms, special education should be viewed in a broader context, within a greater collaborative system of support that works to benefit students with and without IEPs.

Understanding Fear of Change

By a school superintendent

When we started our inclusion journey, our first obstacle was supporting educators and families to better understand why all students would benefit from being fully included in the general education setting. I soon realized that the same staff who were nervous about inclusion had taught parents that these separate rooms and spaces were better. In other words, the traditional view that self-contained classrooms were places where children could receive the highly individualized supports and services they "needed" to be successful was being perpetuated. No amount of research we presented convinced families that their child would flourish in general education. The greatest obstacle we faced was the momentum of over 150 years of segregating students who do not fit into the "typical" student profile. When I took a step back and looked at it from this perspective, it was easy to understand the fear of this change.

1.3: Read and Discuss the Reasons Why People Engage in This Work

We have found that every educator comes to the work of making schools more inclusive for different reasons. Some of the most common reasons are outlined here; understanding them will help you to lead others:

1. **The Research.** Many believe that the research is the most compelling reason to do this work, and rightly so. For decades, research has provided unequivocal evidence that students with and without disabilities do better academically, socially, and behaviorally when educated in inclusive settings (Hehir et al., 2016).

2. **The Law.** Some educators see the law around the least restrictive environment (LRE) and the legal preference for inclusion as reasons to engage in this important work. In the United States, federal law ensures that, "to the maximum extent appropriate, children with disabilities... are educated with children who are not disabled" (Individuals with Disabilities Education Act, 20 U.S.C. 1412[a][5]).
3. **Personal Connections.** Others come to this work because of a personal connection. Perhaps life has created the opportunity for them to advocate long and hard for a child or sibling to be included in general education, or maybe they are moved by the personal story of someone who suffered trauma from being segregated in school. We have heard from many educators who have dedicated their careers to inclusive education because of a powerful personal experience with someone who has a disability.
4. **Caregiver Advocacy.** Still others come to this work because they are pressured to do so by key stakeholders (e.g., family members). At its best, such pressure results in families, advocates, and schools collaborating to support more inclusive efforts. Many school leaders take on the work of inclusion because of due process hearings, mediation, or simply the wishes of caregivers and other advocates.
5. **Social Justice.** Some people see the work from a perspective of ethics and justice. It is well documented that the education profession has made it defensible to segregate large portions of our students based on academic, behavioral, or other membership criteria. Thus, many educators, working to ensure our school systems are equitable, connect to the idea of righting the historical wrong of segregating by disability.
6. **Belonging.** Humans have a basic need to belong, and some view inclusion as a way to create a culture of belonging in a school system. When students feel like they truly belong, they have permission to be their authentic selves, cultivate friendships, build relationships, and experience academic challenges. Structures can either provide all students with access to general education or exclude some students from others. In schools with a culture of belonging, classroom instruction offers multiple ways for students to learn and succeed, building relationships with students is a priority for staff, students' multiple identities are reflected in the curriculum, and families are welcomed and their expertise and ideas are celebrated.

The Research and Inclusive Education

Here, we provide a streamlined summation of the most useful research findings and the most powerful U.S. court cases and legislation related to inclusion. Our hope is that this information will support you in building a strong case to bring others up to speed in terms of the reasons, rationale, and benefits of inclusive education.

Academic Benefits. Studies show that the more time a student with a disability spends in general education, the better that student performs on reading and math assessments (Choi et al., 2017; Cole et al., 2004; Cosier et al., 2013; Dessemontet et al., 2011; Kurth & Mastergeorge, 2010).

The largest longitudinal study of its kind, the National Longitudinal Transition Study (NLTS, 1993; NLTS2, 2004; NLTS2012, 2012), has followed tens of thousands of students with disabilities for decades. Each phase of reporting from this study provides evidence that engagement in general education settings is a critical predictor of academic achievement for students with disabilities (Mazzotti et al., 2021). Specifically, the more general education classes a student is enrolled in, the closer to grade level they are in their reading and math abilities (Wagner et al., 2006).

Schools that are committed to providing systemwide inclusive supports have demonstrated greater student growth on state reading and math assessments than students attending comparable, less-inclusive schools (Choi et al., 2017; Choi et al., 2020).

Social and Behavioral Benefits. When students with disabilities are included in general education, they have fewer disciplinary referrals and miss fewer days of school (Test et al., 2009). They are also more likely to join extracurricular group activities at school and in the community and to regularly see friends outside school (Newman et al., 2010).

The research also shows that students with complex support needs demonstrate increased communication (Foreman et al., 2004) and interpersonal skills (Woodman et al., 2016) and establish a larger network of friendships when they are included in general education classes (Copeland & Cosbey, 2009; Jackson et al., 2008). Additionally, students without disabilities develop a deeper level of acceptance for diversity when they are educated alongside their peers with disabilities (Fisher et al., 2003; Krajewski & Hyde, 2000; Shogren et al., 2015).

Post-Secondary Benefits. Inclusive education is a critical predictor of successful post-secondary experiences for students with disabilities. Students included in general education settings are more likely to graduate high school, access post-secondary education and employment, and live independently (Mazzotti et al., 2021; Test et al., 2009).

Faculty and Staff Benefits. When a school system commits to inclusive education, faculty and staff also benefit. Studies have shown that leaders who provide staff with consistent support systems see an increase in responsive instruction, more sustainable implementation of inclusive practices, and a greater likelihood that educators will feel prepared to collaborate and address the diverse needs of students (Bouillet, 2013; Hehir & Katzman, 2012; Skiba & Losen, 2016).

Educational research has provided clear and consistent evidence for nearly 50 years that inclusion leads to improved outcomes in all areas—academic, social, behavioral, and post-secondary—for students with and without disabilities and regardless of disability label, gender, race, or socioeconomic status.

This robust evidence base for inclusive education alone is compelling enough for most leaders to make an immediate change in service delivery. When paired with the historical path and current legal preference for inclusive education, such a change is practically unavoidable.

The Law and Inclusive Education

The Individuals with Disabilities Education Act (2004), or IDEA, ensures that, "to the maximum extent appropriate, children with disabilities... are educated with children who are not disabled" (Section 1412[a][5]). However, current practices are not reflective of this ideal. Only 65 percent of 6- to 21-year-old students with disabilities spend 80 percent or more of their day in general education classrooms. For students with more complex support needs (e.g., students with autism, intellectual disability, or multiple disabilities), that number drops dramatically to anywhere between 14 percent and 40 percent of students who are included 80 percent or more of their day (National Center for Education Statistics, 2022).

Federal courts in the United States have repeatedly established that inclusive settings are preferable to segregated placements and that special education services are portable. We have provided a summary of important inclusion-related court cases and the impact each has had on the U.S. education system in Figure 1.2. You'll notice that a relatively early court case (1983) determined that "the court should determine whether the services... could be feasibly provided in a non-segregated setting (i.e., regular class). If they can, the placement in the segregated school would be inappropriate under the act (IDEA)" (Roncker v.

Figure 1.2 Important Inclusion-Related Court Cases

Court Case	Outcome
Brown v. Board of Education of Topeka (1954)	The Supreme Court found that racially segregated public schools are inherently unequal. Many in the disability advocacy community apply this concept to segregated schools and settings for students with disabilities. When we think of separate restaurants, drinking fountains, and schools for white and Black people, we can all agree that this type of separation is appalling. Yet in many school systems, we are still comfortable separating students with disabilities from their peers without disabilities.
Pennsylvania Association for Retarded Citizens (PARC) v. Commonwealth of Pennsylvania (1972)	PARC plaintiffs argued that children with intellectual disability (then called "mental retardation") could benefit from educational programs and training. The court ruled that Pennsylvania was responsible for providing free public education to all children; that no child, regardless of their disability, could be turned down; and that the quality of the education provided to children with disabilities needed to match that of their nondisabled peers.
Roncker v. Walter (1983)	This case challenged the placement of students in separate schools and programs. The court ruled in favor of inclusive placements over self-contained settings and established the principle of portability. If a district claims a self-contained placement is superior to an inclusive one, the court should determine if the services offered in the self-contained setting can be feasibly provided in the general education classroom. If they can, then the self-contained setting would be inappropriate under IDEA.
Daniel v. State Board of Education (1989)	The court determined that students with disabilities have a right to be included in both academic and extracurricular programs of general education. The court established a two-part test: first, educators must examine whether the student can be included in general education with the appropriate supplementary aids and services; if not, they must then examine whether the student is included in general education to the maximum extent appropriate.
Oberti v. Board of Education of Clementon School District (1992)	The court ruled that a school did not offer the appropriate supports and services to provide a student with access to inclusive settings. This case established that the burden of proof for compliance with IDEA fell on the school district and state, not the family. The judge stated, "inclusion is a right, not a special privilege for a select few."
Sacramento City Unified School District v. Rachel H. (1994)	The court identified four factors that must be taken into consideration when determining a student's least restrictive environment: (1) the educational benefits of inclusive settings versus segregated settings; (2) nonacademic benefits of interactions between students with and without disabilities; (3) the effect the student with a disability may have on the teacher and classmates; and (4) the cost of services required for the student to access the inclusive setting.
Endrew F. v. Douglas County School District (2017)	In this case, the court clarified the standard of a free, appropriate public education (FAPE) under IDEA. It ruled that the correct standard of FAPE is whether a school district has created an IEP in which the student (1) has challenging and ambitious goals and (2) can make progress according to their own individual needs.
L. H. v. Hamilton County Department of Education (2018)	In this case, the court ruled that the self-contained placement a school provided was more restrictive than necessary and therefore in violation of IDEA. The court also explained that school staff cannot choose to exclude a student from general education simply because they are "unwilling or unable to properly engage in the process of mainstreaming [the student]... rather than isolating and removing him when the situation became challenging."

Walter, 1983, at 1063). It's important to remember that supports and services are easily brought into a general education classroom.

Figure 1.2 also includes newer cases that require students to have access to, be involved in, and make progress in the general education curriculum (Endrew F. v. Douglas, 2017; IDEA, 2004, Section 300.320 [a]). This means that students with disabilities do not have to leave the general education classroom to receive rich individualized special education services and supports. Instead, special education supports and services are brought to the learner in the general education settings—benefiting not only the individual, but all learners and all staff.

Inclusive education has been proven to be so much better for students, educators, and communities. Yet despite the overwhelming evidence, the decades of research, the legal precedents, and the tireless efforts of caregivers and advocates, most leaders still find themselves asking, "How can I change the mindset and culture of our school? How can I get others to buy in and believe in inclusion the way I do?"

1.4: As a Team, Explore Your Personal "Whys"

You came to the work of inclusion for a reason, and you are likely already very committed to and passionate about creating inclusive schools. Clarifying even more the reasons you want to create more inclusive schools will serve you well in leading your system through this change process. You will return to your own "why" and the why of others repeatedly in the journey toward inclusion for all.

If you and your colleagues deeply understand why you are taking this journey, you will feel bolstered to continue through the challenges that may come and be prepared to bring everyone along to your desired outcome. Understanding and committing to the why of this work will ignite your resolve to take the journey and bring you comfort when the trail gets narrow and hard to navigate.

Take a moment here to reflect on your own why as it relates to inclusion and the journey you are embarking upon. Why is the work of equity and inclusive education important to you personally? Why is inclusion a priority now?

Communicate Your Why with Your Team

Gather your trusted leadership team to share your thoughts and ideas with one another. Having an open and honest sharing conversation will help you to develop common reasons why you are working toward inclusion and discuss similarities and differences in your personal rationale. In some districts, everyone writes individual answers on a shared document so that you can easily see your different rationales, hopes and dreams, and priorities for this work. This conversation will solidify the importance and urgency of the work and create even more shared collective purpose for your team.

Rationale at the Ready

By a special education director

When I assumed the role of special education director for a school district with roughly 13,000 students, most students with disabilities were receiving services in self-contained special education classrooms. I knew, based on both research and my experience working in other school systems, that this method was ineffective and needed to be redesigned. Our district's Inclusion Task Force asked the question, "How do we bring services to students rather than bringing students to services?" We engaged in many conversations about how to wrap services around students.

Even with a strong leadership team in place, clear rationale for the change, and a detailed plan of action, questions still arose. Here are some examples:

- Why are we making this change?
- What's wrong with what we've been doing all these years?
- What about the students who "can't handle" general education?
- Can't we do this as a pilot?
- How will we get training?
- What if this doesn't work?

As a leader, I needed to be ready to answer these questions and many more. I also found that for some staff, words were not enough. They needed to see and experience success for themselves firsthand. Others needed time to discuss concerns and revisit what this would mean for them. What it came down to was revisiting our rationale repeatedly. We had to show, share, discuss, and, at times, debate why we were moving toward an inclusive system. We had to have our why at the ready each day.

1.5: Support Leaders Who Continue to Have Questions About Inclusion

Creating shared meaning about your why with your leadership team is a good starting point, but remember, every member of your leadership team will feel different levels of excitement, understanding, readiness, and urgency. Some may arrive at an understanding of their why organically and on their own; others may be led to it by you or may feel pushed, rushed, or resistant. To support everyone, you will need to spend time with them to understand their concerns and fears, hopes and dreams, and strengths.

Loop Ahead: We will discuss more about supporting people through change in Chapter 7. If getting everyone on your leadership team on the same path to inclusion is a significant obstacle for you, jump ahead to Chapter 7 to get more strategies and ideas.

A Little Bit Softer Now

We have seen leaders try to convince others of their inclusive why by simply offering up more facts, figures, and information. It makes logical sense—to us. When someone is resistant or hesitant, we tend to turn up the dial by giving them more data, more reasons, more arguments, and even more training to help them "come around." But believe it or not, this approach can lead to more pushback, more resistance, and more inertia (Berger, 2020).

Understanding what triggers those individuals or makes them feel unsafe allows us to address their resistance with more compassion and understanding. Our goal is to give people a sense of agency and safety and to reduce barriers and remove challenges in their way.

Ask questions that start with *why, how,* and *what,* because these types of questions offer hope and possibility and highlight room for growth. By contrast, *who, where, which,* and *yes/no* questions can be limiting.

You can use the following questions to guide your conversations:

- What fears or worries do you have about moving in an inclusive direction?
- How can I help you overcome the challenges you face?

- What resources will you need to achieve your goals?

This chapter was designed to help you clarify and communicate your rationale and personal why around inclusive education. You had the opportunity to explore an equity lens as well as how to develop shared meaning and purpose about inclusion with your leadership team. We provided common examples of the whys of other leaders as well as a detailed overview of inclusion-related research and legal decisions in the United States. Now that you've completed this chapter, we invite you to gather your leadership team and reflect on the Milestone 1 leadership questions and steps together.

Milestone 1: Do we understand why inclusive education is the way forward?
Leadership Questions **Q 1.1** Is the leadership team clear on what inclusion means? **Q 1.2** Do we understand the equity lens? **Q 1.3** How will the leadership team explore their own "why"? **Q 1.4** Does the leadership team know how to communicate why inclusion is the way forward?
Leadership Steps **S 1.1** Develop a shared understanding of inclusive education. **S 1.2** Explore the equity lens together. **S 1.3** Read and discuss the reasons why people engage in this work. **S 1.4** As a team, explore your personal "whys." **S 1.5** Support leaders who continue to have questions about inclusion.

Consider your team's discussion around these questions and steps: Where is there clarity and where might your team need to focus additional time and energy? Then, turn to your Action Plan and add any necessary steps.

Your Action Plan

Go to your Action Plan. If you haven't created yours yet, you can use the template in Appendix A (p. 113) or access one at www.inclusiveschooling.com/the-way-to-inclusion or www.ascd.org/the-way-to-inclusion-resources. With your leadership team, add any necessary action steps for your system.

2

See the System

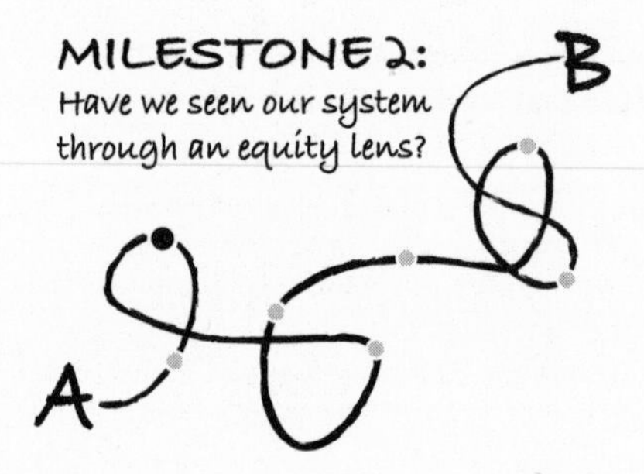

This milestone is at the heart of inclusive system change. To develop an intentionally designed, inclusive learning community, leaders must be willing to look critically and honestly at their current system. Such analysis is brave and at times uncomfortable work. Seeing your system through the lens of equity can feel challenging because it causes us to reflect on what we as leaders have either created or inherited. But we are not here to shame or blame. Rather, we want you to know that we, the authors, have *all* been in your position, sitting with the realization that a system was not designed to serve all students in the way we know that it can and should. If we want a system where all students belong, we need to first understand the current reality.

Equity Review Data Collection Guide

This chapter is all about the work needed to conduct an equity review of your system with a focus on special education. Central to that review is the Equity Review Data Collection Guide, or Data Guide for short (Causton & MacLeod,

2022a) in Appendix B (p. 114). Take a moment now to acquaint yourself with this document.

The Data Guide will help you to gather all the data you'll need to analyze your system so you can name and address any current inequities. It will take you through a thorough qualitative and quantitative exploration of your system-level data, which you will apply in subsequent chapters. In this chapter, we explain how to analyze the collected data and provide visual examples to help you best understand the full process and share tips from administrators who have traveled this path before you. At the end of the chapter, we ask you to review and discuss this milestone's leadership questions and steps to determine your Action Plan steps.

2.1: Collect Your System Equity Data

To begin this equity review, your leadership team will need to collect qualitative and quantitative system-level data. The quantitative data will include, but need not be limited to, information related to student demographics, student placement, staff allocation, roles, schedules, caseloads, student achievement, and discipline. The qualitative data will include, but again need not be limited to, classroom observations, a "day in the life" observation of a student, and focus groups with diverse system community members. In this section, we take you through the Data Guide piece by piece and explain briefly how to analyze each set of collected data.

The data in Figure 2.1 (p. 28) tells you where your students are educated (in general education, in separate settings, etc.) as well as how many staff members you have and how you are using them. This data is some of your most important system-change information. The least restrictive environment (LRE) data will help you to see how often schools separate students. The staffing data will help you to draw your service-delivery maps later in this chapter, so you can see if you are already using staff inclusively or if they are clustered in separate spaces and programs. Staffing titles and positions are important because they help you clarify how your system uses specific language to identify student supports (e.g., *resource, co-teach, life skills*). We ask you to count the number of paraprofessionals in your system, knowing that there are many common terms for this position (e.g., teaching assistants, aides, 1:1 educational assistants, instructional assistants, educational technicians).

The data in Figure 2.2 (p. 29) helps you to understand the over- or underrepresentation of students living in poverty in special education

Figure 2.1 Equity Review Data Collection Guide: General System Demographic Data

1. Number of total students in the system	
2. Number and percentage of students with IEPs in the system	
3. LRE data for the system	80% or more in general education: 40–79% in general education: Less than 40% in general education: In district school outside of home building: Out of district:
4. Number of special education teachers at each school and their special education positions/titles (e.g., resource teacher, self-contained teacher, co-teacher, resource/co-teacher)	
5. Number of general education teachers at each school	
6. Number of related service providers (e.g., OT, PT, SLP, psychologist) and specialists (e.g., literacy, math, multilingual language, gifted and talented) at each school	
7. Number of special education paraprofessionals at each school and specific positions/titles (you can also include the number of non–special education paraprofessionals)	

Source: Causton, J., & MacLeod, K. (2022a). *Equity Review Data Collection Guide,* Inclusive Schooling.

in your system—what's known as *disproportionality*. If, say, 40 percent of students in your system qualify for free or reduced-price lunch, then roughly 40 percent of your students with IEPs should also qualify for it.

To determine if disproportionality is present in your system, divide the outcome percentage of a certain group by the outcome percentage of the whole. For example, if 40 percent of your overall student population qualifies for free or reduced-price lunch, but 80 percent of your students with IEPs do, this means that students who receive free or reduced-price lunch are two times as likely as the general population to be identified as requiring special education. You can further analyze disproportionality using building-level data.

Figure 2.2 Student Socioeconomic Data

8. Number and percentage of students who qualify for free or reduced-price lunch in the system	
9. Number and percentage of students with IEPs who qualify for free or reduced-price lunch	
10. Number and percentage of students with IEPs in specific LRE categories who qualify for free or reduced-price lunch	80% or more in general education: 40–79% in general education: Less than 40% in general education: In district school outside of home building: Out of district:

The data in Figure 2.3 (p. 30) helps you to understand the disproportional representation of students of color in special education in your system. To determine if disproportionality is present, divide the outcome percentage of a specific racial or ethnic group by the outcome percentage of a whole. For example, if 15 percent of your overall student population is African American, but 35 percent of your students with IEPs are, this means African American students are more than two times as likely as the general population to be identified as requiring special education.

Figure 2.3 Student Race or Ethnicity Data

Note: Though race and ethnicity are separate constructs, both are reflected in the categories used by the U.S. Office of Special Education to request and track specific student demographic data.

11. Number and percentage of students of color in your system (broken down by race or ethnicity)	
12. Number and percentage of students of color in your system with IEPs (broken down by race or ethnicity)	
13. Number and percentage of students of color with IEPs in specific LRE categories	80% or more in general education: 40–79% in general education: Less than 40% in general education: In district school outside of home building: Out of district:

The data in Figure 2.4 helps you to understand the disproportional representation of students with specific disabilities in special education in your system. For example, you can identify if students with specific disability labels are disproportionately placed in more restrictive settings, or if students of specific racial or ethnic groups are disproportionately labeled with specific disabilities. To determine disproportionality, divide the outcome percentage for a specific group (e.g., African American students with intellectual disability) by the outcome percentage of the whole (e.g., students with intellectual disability). For example, if 8 percent of your overall student population is labeled as having an intellectual disability, but 15 percent of African American students are labeled as having an intellectual disability, this means that African American students are nearly twice as likely as the general population to be labeled with an intellectual disability.

The data in Figure 2.5 will help you to understand your system's student achievement data broken down by specific student populations. For example, you can identify which student groups are graduating at the highest or lowest rates. You can further analyze this data for disproportionality and student intersectionality.

Figure 2.4 Disability Label Data

14. Number of students with specific disability labels in your system; you can further break this data down by demographic category (e.g., students with IEPs, race/ethnicity, eligibility for free or reduced-price lunch, multilingual learners)	
15. Number of students with specific disability labels in specific LRE categories; you can further break this data down by demographic category (e.g., students with IEPs, race/ethnicity, eligibility for free or reduced-price lunch, multilingual learners)	80% or more in general education: 40–79% in general education: Less than 40% in general education: In district school outside of home building: Out of district:

Figure 2.5 Achievement Data

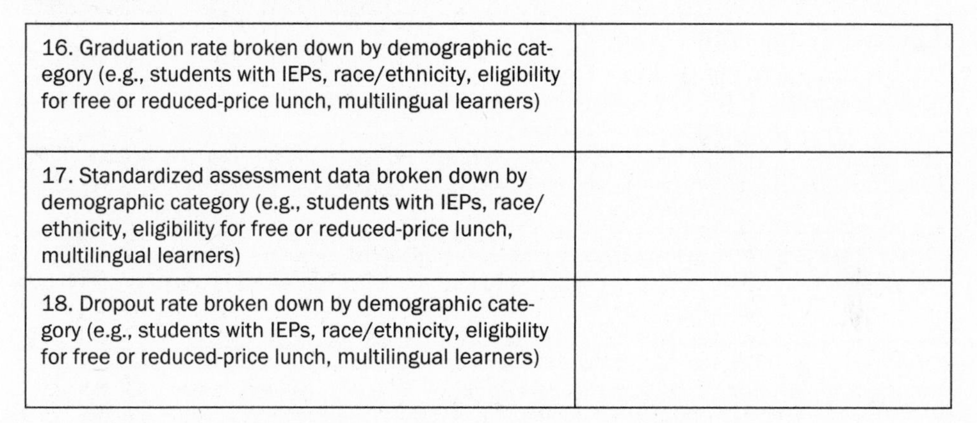

16. Graduation rate broken down by demographic category (e.g., students with IEPs, race/ethnicity, eligibility for free or reduced-price lunch, multilingual learners)	
17. Standardized assessment data broken down by demographic category (e.g., students with IEPs, race/ethnicity, eligibility for free or reduced-price lunch, multilingual learners)	
18. Dropout rate broken down by demographic category (e.g., students with IEPs, race/ethnicity, eligibility for free or reduced-price lunch, multilingual learners)	

The data in Figure 2.6 (p. 32) will help you to understand your system's behavioral data broken down by specific student populations. For example, you can identify which student groups are disciplined at the highest and lowest rates. To determine if disproportionality is present, divide the outcome percentage of a specific group (e.g., students with IEPs) by the outcome percentage of the whole. For example, if 10 percent of your overall student population received out-of-school suspensions but 20 percent of students with IEPs did, this means that students with IEPs are two times as likely as the general population to receive out-of-school suspensions. You can further analyze disproportionality by student groups at every building for a more comprehensive look at discipline across your system.

Figure 2.6 Behavioral Data

19. Number of disciplinary actions (by type) for all students in the system	
20. Number of disciplinary actions (by type) broken down by demographic category (e.g., students with IEPs, race/ethnicity, eligibility for free or reduced-price lunch, multilingual learners)	

Once your leadership team has collected the quantitative data described thus far, you will need to collect qualitative data (see Figure 2.7) to get an understanding of on-the-ground practices and community understanding of inclusion and equity.

Figure 2.7 Qualitative Data

Classroom Visits	The leadership team can conduct classroom visits of all educational settings to better understand how staff is used in each classroom and what instructional practices occur. We recommend using the Inclusive Classroom Observation Tool in Appendix C (p. 118) to maintain consistent observational data.
A Day in the Life of a Student	Each member of the leadership team can select a student and compile qualitative data about what that student experiences in a single school day—anything from social and hallway experiences to classroom instructional practices, types of adult support, or even time spent in or out of general education. It is helpful for the team to select diverse students in terms of disability, race/ethnicity, language, gender expression, and age. One district we worked with had staff (and students) identify students who were thriving in the system. They studied factors that contributed to their success to increase opportunities for all.
Surveys and/or Focus Groups	The leadership team can share a survey with the system community members and/or hold focus groups with staff, families, and students. This data collection helps the leadership team to understand how these diverse groups understand inclusion practices, structures, and supports. We recommend using the Inclusive System Focus Group Survey in Appendix D (p. 120) to guide you or create your own.

Once you have gathered this qualitative data, you will analyze it to better understand (1) how staff are used across educational settings, (2) what instructional practices are used across educational settings, (3) the lived school experiences of students, and (4) the ways diverse community members understand the meaning of inclusion and the current use of inclusive structures and practices in your system.

The Equity Review Data Collection Guide is at the heart of the inclusive education change process, but there is certainly additional system data that your leadership team may want to collect and analyze depending on your system's unique needs. Systems that have a large population of multilingual learners, for example, or educators interested in understanding gender representation in special education, can use a similar data collection and analysis approach as the one in the Data Guide.

2.2: Visually Represent System Equity Data Using Graphs or Charts

Creating visual representations of collected system data helps your leadership team to analyze the data more easily. Figure 2.8 provides an example of student LRE data for a school system and is further broken down by building. This type of visualization helps you to clearly identify the LRE trends for specific schools in your system, sometimes pointing to building-level differences in staff beliefs and practices or clusters of separate programs in a single building.

Figure 2.8 Sample Student LRE Data for All Students with IEPs in a School System

	Total Students with IEPs	80–100% of the Day in Gen. Ed.	40–79% of the Day in Gen. Ed.	0–39% of the Day in Gen. Ed.	Separate School/Out of District
District	20%	48%	27%	16%	9%
Elem. 1	14%	70%	6%	19%	5%
Elem. 2	24%	33%	63%	1%	3%
Elem. 3	19%	40%	5%	47 %	8%
Middle School	17.5%	57%	24%	16%	3%
High School	17%	62%	33%	0%	5%

Figure 2.9 shows the student LRE data for an entire school system broken down by demographic. This type of visualization helps you to clearly identify any disproportionality in the ways specific groups of students are included in or excluded from general education settings.

Figure 2.9 Sample Data Visualization: Table

Demographics	80–100% of the Day in Gen. Ed.	40–79% of the Day in Gen. Ed.	0–39% of the Day in Gen. Ed.	Separate School/Out of District
All Students	48%	27%	16%	9%
White	50%	30%	12%	8%
African American	17%	69%	7%	7%
Hispanic/Latino	43%	37%	5%	15%
Multiracial	53%	30%	5%	12%
Eligibility for Free or Reduced-Price Lunch	47%	35%	16%	2%

Note: Student demographic groups with fewer than 11 students enrolled in special education services are not included in this table.

Figure 2.10 shows student discipline data related to out-of-school suspensions (OSS) for an entire school system broken down by demographic category. This type of visualization helps you to clearly identify disproportionality in the ways specific groups of students are disciplined. For example, the data in Figure 2.10 shows that white students are underrepresented in this system's discipline data, making up 62 percent of the general student population but only 19 percent of its OSS recipients. By contrast, African American students and students with disabilities (SWD) are overrepresented, with African American students 4.5 times more likely to receive an OSS and SWD twice as likely to receive one than their peers in the general population.

Figure 2.10 Sample Data Visualization: Bar Chart

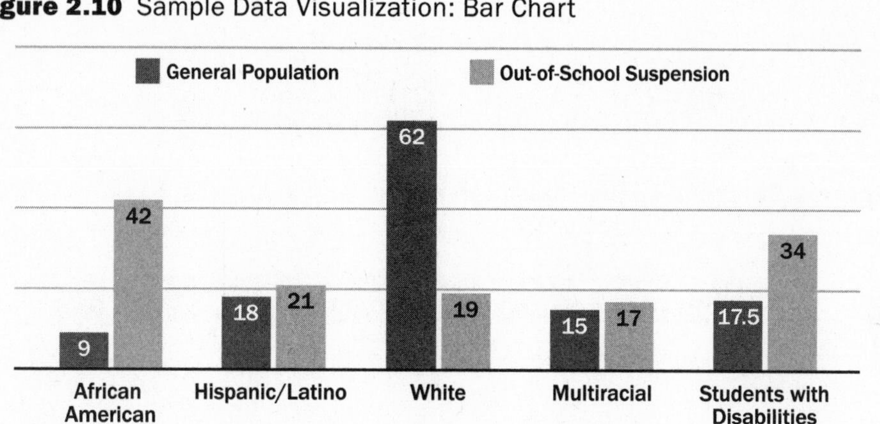

Your leadership team can continue to visualize system data in the ways we've outlined in this chapter. Even if you're stumped about how best to represent the qualitative data, we recommend at the very least summarizing key findings and including them in a succinct slide deck that you can share easily.

2.3: Create Building-Level Service-Delivery Maps

Using the general system demographic data you've collected, your leadership team should next draw building-level service-delivery maps to visualize how your system uses staffing and structures. When we work with districts, we like to first create a key like the one in Figure 2.11 (p. 36).

Your leadership team can add to this key. For example, you may want to include an image to represent related service providers or specialists such as gifted and talented, literacy, math, or multilingual teachers. Figures 2.12 (p. 36), 2.13 (p. 37), and 2.14 (p. 37) show examples of service-delivery maps for the elementary, middle, and high school buildings of a system in which we worked.

Figure 2.11 Service-Delivery Map Key

General Education Teacher	Special Education Teacher	Paraprofessional

Figure 2.12 Sample Elementary Service-Delivery Map

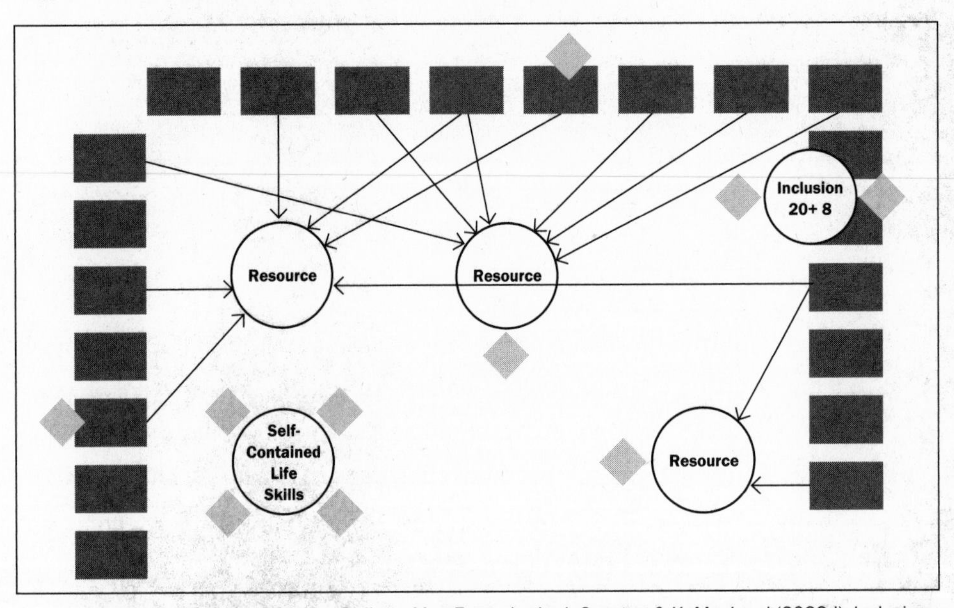

Source: From *Inclusive Reform Service-Delivery Map Examples* by J. Causton & K. MacLeod (2022d), Inclusive Schooling. Copyright 2022 by Inclusive Schooling. Reprinted with permission.

Loop Ahead: You might be curious to see how this school district analyzed their maps and realigned service delivery to create new inclusive maps. Loop ahead to Chapter 4 to see their before and after maps. In Chapter 4, we take you through realigning your before maps as well.

Figure 2.13 Sample Middle School Service-Delivery Map

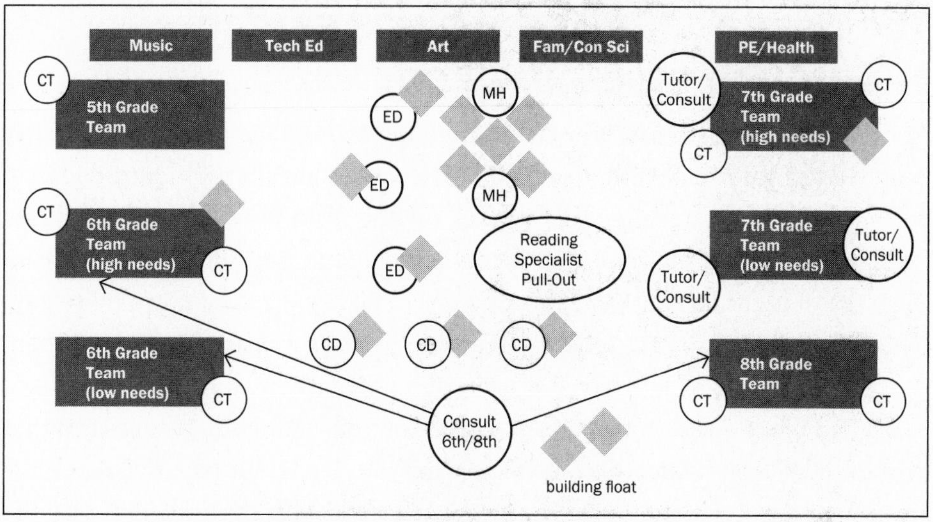

Music
Tech Ed
Art
Fam/Con Sci
PE/Health
CT
5th Grade Team
ED
MH
Tutor/ Consult
7th Grade Team (high needs)
CT
CT
ED
MH
CT
6th Grade Team (high needs)
CT
ED
Reading Specialist Pull-Out
7th Grade Team (low needs)
Tutor/ Consult
Tutor/ Consult
CD
CD
CD
6th Grade Team (low needs)
CT
8th Grade Team
CT
CT
Consult 6th/8th
building float

Source: From *Inclusive Reform Service-Delivery Map Examples* by J. Causton & K. MacLeod (2022d), Inclusive Schooling. Copyright 2022 by Inclusive Schooling. Reprinted with permission.

Figure 2.14 Sample High School Service-Delivery Map

CT & Resource
12th Grade
CT-CTE & Resource
CTE
CT
Tutor Pullout & Push-In
9th Grade Team 1
9th Grade Resource
CT
9th Grade Team 2
9th Grade Team 3 (Hon)
Tutor Pullout
Tutor Pullout
MH
MH
CT & Resource
CT & Resource
11th Grade
CT & Resource
Alt Ed
Alt Ed
10th Grade Team 1
10th Grade Team 2
CT & Resource
CT & Resource
Electives
10th Grade Team 3 (Hon)

Source: From *Inclusive Reform Service-Delivery Map Examples* by J. Causton & K. MacLeod (2022d), Inclusive Schooling. Copyright 2022 by Inclusive Schooling. Reprinted with permission.

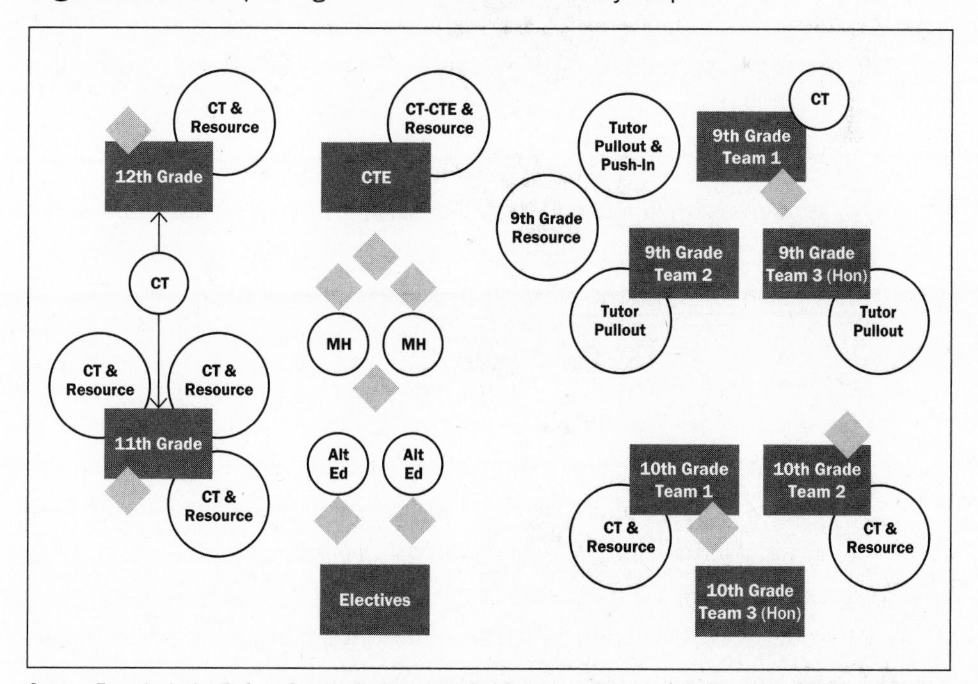

2.4: Share the System Data with the Leadership Team and Analyze It Through an Equity Lens

Your leadership team can now spend time reviewing the data using an equity lens. Gather your leadership team and review the data chart by chart and map by map, or perhaps create a gallery walk for the team to review different data sets posted around the room. We highly recommend that the leadership team view the data for the entire district before breaking the data down by school. This is an opportunity for school and district leaders to learn from each other.

Data should not be viewed as punitive but, rather, as an opportunity to learn and move closer to your ideal vision for your students. It is critical that you, as the leader, model this perspective for your leadership team. The leaders in your system are watching to see how you engage with the data. Embrace the data as your current reality, allowing you to see patterns in your system and identify areas of growth to help you move toward greater inclusion. Following are some ideas to guide your work with your team.

Examine Placement and LRE Data

As a starting point, examine existing placement and LRE data for students with disabilities using an equity lens. Leaders should look for patterns that could be driving inequitable practices and segregation of students. Consider the following questions when reviewing this data:

- Are inclusive placements only considered for some students?
- Are students with labels sent to separate programs in separate spaces?
- Do students with specific labels go to certain programs (e.g., autism program, behavior program, multiple disabilities program)?
- Do we believe the best place to serve students with specific labels is in those specific programs?
- Do students with specific labels get greater access to the general education content and experiences than other students with different labels?
- Is "remove and remediate" part of the general belief around how to best educate students who perform differently or not at grade level in your system?
- Do students with disabilities have to leave their siblings and their neighbors to attend schools not in their neighborhood catchment area?

If the answer to any of these questions is "Yes," leaders must examine the attitudinal and structural barriers in their systems that are leading to these beliefs and practices.

Examine Service-Delivery Maps

Next, leaders can examine existing service-delivery maps through an equity lens. This means looking for patterns that emerge that could be driving inequitable practices and segregation of students. Consider the following questions when reviewing service-delivery maps:

- Are staff clustered in certain rooms (e.g., autism program, behavior program, multiple disabilities program)?
- Do some grade levels or classrooms have inclusive support while others do not?
- Are special educators too busy staffing resource rooms, life skills rooms, and behavioral rooms to support students inclusively in general education?
- Are paraprofessionals frequently used to support special education programs and classes?

If the answer to any of these questions is "Yes," leaders must further examine the attitudinal and structural barriers in their systems that are leading to these beliefs and practices.

Examine Qualitative Data

Leaders will next want to review classroom observation data, focus group and/or survey data, and "day in the life" data. Leaders should look for patterns that emerge that relate to attitudes, practices, and structures that could be driving segregation of students. Consider the following questions when reviewing qualitative data:

- What are the attitudes and beliefs about inclusive education in the system?
- What patterns emerge when instructional practices across various educational settings are compared? For example, do the same types of instructional practices occur in general education classrooms and in resource classrooms?
- How are adults used in classrooms? Do teachers and paraprofessionals support all students or only specific groups of students?

The answers to these questions will help you to identify areas of strength and need as it relates to your staff beliefs, attitudes, and inclusive instructional practices.

Take Time to Discuss System Bias

Once you have examined demographic and staffing data and determined if certain groups of students are disproportionately educated in restrictive placements, a much larger discussion needs to occur. Often, these inequities exist due to systemic beliefs, practices, and policies that are racist, ableist, classist, and so on. To address these harmful practices, leaders can simultaneously use the IEP process to create inclusive change and move away from any reliance on separate placements and programs.

2.5: Name and Take Action to Remedy Inequities in the Current System

Exploring, naming, and documenting systemwide inequities helps your leadership team to gain clarity on what the equity review and discussion has revealed about your current system. We have found that these inequities are most easily explained as "key findings" from the system equity review. Here are some examples:

- Leaders and staff are committed to inclusion but want training and support.
- There is an overreliance on separate programming for students with IEPs.
- African American students with IEPs are disproportionately at risk for suspension.
- Students of color are disproportionately represented in self-contained settings.
- Paraprofessionals are clustered in separate special education classrooms and programs.

These findings become the catalyst to move you toward inclusive change in your system. In fact, you will use the key findings from your equity review to form your inclusive vision and rationale in Chapter 3.

This chapter was designed to guide you through a comprehensive equity review of your system data. Committing to truly seeing your system is a critical step in the inclusive change process, so congratulations! Now that you've completed this chapter, we invite you to gather your leadership team and reflect on the Milestone 2 leadership questions and steps together.

Milestone 2: Have we seen our system through an equity lens?
Leadership Questions **Q 2.1** Which students are not educated within their home school or home school district? **Q 2.2** Which students do not have access to general education classrooms, content, and peers for most of the day? **Q 2.3** Which students are over- or underrepresented in special education, in more restrictive placements, or in terms of disciplinary action? **Q 2.4** Which students are still in separate programs or classrooms for students with specific disabilities? **Q 2.5** Do educators and related service providers work in collaborative teams? **Q 2.6** Do any special educators or related service providers work in separate rooms, spaces, or programs?
Leadership Steps **S 2.1** Collect system data using the Equity Review Data Collection Guide. **S 2.2** Visually represent system equity data using graphs or charts. **S 2.3** Create building-level service-delivery maps. **S 2.4** Share the system data with the leadership team and analyze it through an equity lens. **S 2.5** Name and take action to remedy inequities in the current system.

Consider your team's discussion around these questions and steps: Where is there clarity and where might your team need to focus additional time and energy? Then, turn to your Action Plan and add any necessary steps.

ACTION PLAN

Your Action Plan

Go to your Action Plan and record any necessary action steps.

3

Develop Your Inclusive Vision

MILESTONE 3:
Do we have a clear public vision for inclusion and understanding of the needed system-level changes?

A

B

This chapter sets the stage for understanding why leaders need to create and communicate an aspirational, clear, and actionable vision. In any system, many beliefs and values are written and spoken, while others are hidden or unspoken. All these beliefs and values require close examination in order to challenge longstanding practices that have led to inequitable structures for students, including those with disabilities.

In this chapter, we discuss what a vision statement is and who is involved in creating it. We also provide examples of inclusive vision statements from other districts. We share how providing a rationale for any vision work is necessary and suggest ways to share your vision with all stakeholders. Lastly, we describe innovative ways leaders have created and shared their visions and navigated specific challenges.

What We Mean by *Vision*

When we refer to a school system's vision, we are referencing a concise and powerful set of spoken or written statements that reflect the collective beliefs, values, and goals of those who work in and are served by the school system. These statements can be labeled vision statements, mission statements, or even promises. They are often shared publicly on websites and during school board and staff meetings and even decorate the halls of many school buildings. Great leaders help all members of a school system to understand these statements, put them into practice, support one another, and provide accountability.

The People Involved

The success of this undertaking cannot and should not rely on one person alone. This is particularly true when shifting the vision and purpose of education toward inclusivity. Because the assumptions that underlie segregated special education practices are deeply entrenched in the cultures of schools, distributing leadership and finding individuals to serve as ambassadors for inclusive vision work is critical to sustainable change.

We recommend establishing a guiding committee—an "Inclusion Task Force," for example, or an "Inclusive Steering Committee"—to share leadership tasks central to keeping the goal of inclusive education at the forefront of any systemwide change efforts. We also suggest that you involve your leadership team and others who are innovative thinkers, who are inclusivity-oriented, and who represent the diversity of humans working within and served by your school system. Most important, be sure to include representative families and students on this guiding committee.

Create Balanced Committees

By a director of special education

The initial makeup of our inclusion steering committee skewed toward special education staff and administrators. We struggled to recruit general educators and leaders, who tended to see the work of the committee as a special education initiative rather than a systemwide effort. To get more balance and achieve greater representation of our staff, we took some critical steps. First, we shifted from monthly to quarterly meetings, which enticed more general educators to attend. We also combined our efforts with other school-based committees to reduce the number of groups that had to meet and tasks that needed our attention. We then had everyone on the committee invite building-level leaders and instructional specialists to join. While we continue to work for more balance, we have recognized that a few creative decisions allowed us to get essential feedback and collaboration from all perspectives.

Loop Back: Bring your leadership team's shared meaning of inclusion (from Chapter 1) and system equity data (from Chapter 2) to your visioning work. These components are critical to the work of revising or drafting your system's inclusivity vision statement.

3.1: Craft or Revise a Vision Statement

Whether working from an existing vision statement or drafting a new one, we recommend that you begin your work with the shared definition of inclusion you have created and your system's equity data at the ready. You want the vision to boldly align with your definition of inclusion and address the systemic inequities that may exist for students with marginalized identities in your system. Consider how your vision can function as a catalyst for change. Here, for example, is an example of a vision statement from a district that took its leadership team's definition of inclusion and identified inclusive practices and structures to implement:

> We establish practices and structures that support our diverse community of learners as they learn together in general education classrooms. Our decision making is student centered and our staff work collaboratively to support all learners. We intentionally differentiate our curriculum to celebrate and support individual students. We provide humanistic and compassionate support to all students to increase their sense of belonging and create an inclusive school climate. Staff work to support all student learning using a variety of entry points to create greater access, inspire greater engagement, and lead to greater success for all learners.

Once you draft or revise your vision statement, we recommend analyzing each sentence separately by asking the following questions:

- What does our vision say? What do we think that means?
- Do we have sentences that clearly promote inclusive educational practices?

- Do we have sentences that identify the inclusive values we stand for?
- Do we have sentences that address systemic inequities for our students?

The purpose of the vision statement is to help define your inclusive dreams and move your system forward, so some leaders opt to include actionable and measurable goals in their statements. Here is an example of a vision that has an embedded measurable action (in bold):

> We deeply believe that our collective differences are our greatest strength. Here, we celebrate the fact that every classroom and grade level has a broad range of learners. We draw upon differences to educate our students together. We no longer accept that some students belong in separate spaces or places. **We will have all students supported inclusively in general education classrooms and benefiting from collaborative educator support and differentiated learning experiences within two school years.**

Whether your vision is actionable like this one or more aspirational like the previous example, you will need to explain how the vision came to be. In the next section, we ask you to analyze your system data and your vision statement side by side to ensure you can articulate why this work is necessary to a broad audience.

3.2: Develop a Clear Rationale Using Key Findings from Your System Equity Review

Use the key findings from your system equity review to develop a clear rationale for your vision (see Figure 3.1 on p. 46 for an example).

Hold a "Data Day"

By a special education director

To make staff aware of the inequities that exist in our schools and district, we had a "data day" during which we looked at and analyzed academic achievement data, placement practices, and social-emotional learning data. Building teams met and reviewed graphs and charts that illustrated the data broken down by disability labels, percentage of time included with general education peers, and whether students had IEPs.

When analyzing the data, we were able to specify which students with which disability labels were currently being segregated. We could see how placement practices affected academic achievement, and we began to hypothesize about the mindset, policies, systems, and structures that were leading to segregation.

The data also revealed exemplary practices within our system that were improving academic outcomes for both students with IEPs and students without IEPs. We then studied these successful teams, grades, and buildings in more detail to learn what they were doing and apply those practices to increasing the strength of the overall system.

Our "data day" also gave educators a chance to identify other areas worthy of celebration. It naturally built a sense of urgency to identify inequities and to share a clear rationale for the necessity of this journey toward inclusion.

Figure 3.1 Template for Vision Rationale Using Equity Review Key Findings

We are doing this work because

- We are out of LRE compliance for [number] ______ students.
- We have [number] ______ students out of district.
- [Demographic group] ______ students are overrepresented in special education and in separate settings.
- We have life skills classes in [number] ______ schools and those students are not meaningfully included.
- We want educators to collaborate with each other rather than work in separate spaces.
- Educators are interested in inclusion but have requested additional support from leaders.
- Many families have asked to have their children meaningfully included in general education and we have gone to mediation with [number] ______ families and due process with [number] ______ families.
- Students who have autism are bused to an entirely different school. We believe that is not fair, equitable, or legal.
- Students of color and economically disadvantaged students are significantly underrepresented in our talented and gifted program. (Ratio) ______.

3.3: Get Feedback on the Vision from Diverse Members of the School System

Getting feedback from diverse individuals in your system elevates the visioning process by granting the entire system ownership of it. Take the time to learn from those who have been marginalized by the system to understand how the language and ideas currently in use may be outdated or discriminatory. Learn what language should be used instead and what actions are needed to repair harm. Because race is always at play in the work we do and students of color are overrepresented in special education, receive more restrictive placements, and are disciplined more often than their white peers, it is important to examine your vision for areas where white cultural norms and bias may be affecting the work. Then, partner with students, families, colleagues, and experts of color to revise. Including a diverse group of school system members is critical for making sure your vision is a vision for everyone.

A Promise Statement

By a school superintendent

As we began the critical work of developing a new strategic plan for our district, we also agreed to review our commitment to our vision and mission. We sought out staff, students, families, and community members to help us determine the path forward. After many conversations, the team decided to move away from a vision statement and adopt a promise statement instead. Our students were the driving force behind this decision. They said a promise spoke to them directly and felt personal, concrete, and attainable.

As the voices of staff, families, students, and community members came alive, it was clear that our district had worked well for some students but not all. Specifically, students who were Hispanic/Latino, identified as LGBTQ+, had an IEP, and/or received free or reduced-price lunch were unlikely to thrive in our schools. We needed to create space for honest reflections about our district before developing a promise that would positively impact everyone in the district.

Our students spoke about the lack of diversity among staff, in upper-level courses, and in student organizations. The team discussed how equity is about having high expectations for each student, no matter their address, ability, or background, and then supporting each student to meet these expectations.

After months of conversations, the team created our promise statement:

> We promise to develop a foundation of diversity, equity, and inclusion from which each student emerges future-ready.

The rationale behind each word held great importance for the team. We knew our promise had to begin with building a new foundation focused on diversity, equity, and inclusion. Our students demanded that diversity, equity, and inclusion (DEI) concerns be integral to the promise statement. Though many adults tried to moderate the statement's language, our students insisted we explicitly reference DEI and educate people as to why it is critical for the future-readiness of our students. Our promise is the foundation of our work, and there are many different aspects that will make it come alive.

Include a Representative Set of Administrators

Whether you call your dream for your district a vision or a promise, central office and building leadership should be involved in crafting it. Central office leaders tend to have a global lens on the organization, while building administrators are the leaders who will implement the change daily and have insight into what strategies will work at the site level. Building- and district-level administrators need to be on the same page. Comments such as "Central office told us that we're doing inclusion now" or "If only the principals did what we asked" communicate a lack of trust and belief in inclusion to staff, students, and families. Central office and building leaders must stand strongly together and support one another.

3.4: Share the Finalized Vision and Rationale Widely

Once the vision is ready, it's time for it to be shared more widely. All leaders, staff, and community members must understand the vision, commit to breathing life into it, and be accountable to it. We encourage each school and district to develop a thoughtful communication plan for sharing the vision. It is important to think through the timing of messages and when different groups will receive the information. We always suggest that the board of education and the staff hear the message and plans first. When they are clear on the direction, it is time to share the following with all families and students and solicit feedback from them:

- A clear definition of inclusion
- A clear and inclusive vision
- A rationale for the vision based on key findings from your system equity review
- Examples of what becoming an inclusive school system will mean for staff, students, and families

- How staff, students, and families will be supported through the change process
- How all system members will receive updates and how input will be obtained

Effective communication skills are vital for leaders on this journey. Laying out a detailed vision of the work ahead for the board, staff, families, and students is critical. The moment the school or district begins the change process toward greater inclusion, leaders will need to ensure that they've thought through many of the questions that will be asked and are prepared with thoughtful answers.

A Listening Tour

By a special education director

Once we had crafted our vision, we embarked on a nearly 20-school "tour" across the district to share it at every building's faculty meeting. We made sure every single group heard the same clear and concise message. Our message included both our "why" and our vision, highlighting key findings from the data. We also shared our next steps and what these steps would mean for staff, students, and families. Lastly, we answered questions and provided listening sessions.

Though this process was labor intensive, it demonstrated to each person that this effort was important and supported by the upper levels of administration. It allowed each school to ask questions in an intimate environment and communicated the vision from a single source rather than filtering it through scores of building administrators.

Stay as Long as It Takes

A director of special education in a small district jokingly called her listening tour "the road show." She attributed her success with inclusive system change to her philosophy of "staying as long as it takes." She would stay and answer questions with any group until they simply had no more questions and everyone was reasonably satisfied with the answers. Or, if she ran out of time, she would reschedule and show up again and again—as long as it took. These consistent and repeated opportunities for conversation with school system members made her one of the most successful school change leaders we have ever seen. Her school district has moved from 21 self-contained classrooms for students with disabilities to only 2. This year, she is working on closing those remaining rooms and ensuring that the students in them are meaningfully included.

Create a Q&A Document

Another way we recommend supporting districts is by creating a living Q&A document online where questions people ask can be recorded along with responses and links to the research or legal underpinning to support the responses. Organizing questions into categories (e.g., general questions about inclusion, questions about related services, questions about academic instruction) and creating a linked table of contents can help people to quickly find answers to their questions.

Establish How the Vision Will Be Used

Clarify to the community that the vision statement isn't just another slogan but, rather, a driving force behind all system decisions that will function as an accountability measure for systemwide change. Showing how the vision statement will be used, how it represents the values of the larger community, and how accountability is built into it will provide clarity.

A Decision-Making Tool

By an inclusive schooling expert

When working alongside a school principal, I noticed the hundreds of on-the-fly decisions she was making in a single day. For example, on the day of my visit, a teacher had come by to discuss the need for pull-out instruction for a group of students. The teacher was asking permission to pull a select group of students out of their reading block to receive more targeted reading intervention. The principal thought to herself, "Well, it's only a few kids. It will be fine."

She later reflected on that decision and said she made it due to decision fatigue. She shared that she wanted a simple tool to keep her centered on her vision in the face of all the questions coming at her throughout the day. So we worked together to create what she called her "Inclusive Decision-Making Tool":

Does this idea...

- Fit our commitment to inclusion?
- Create a sense of belonging for more students?
- Make our school structures more inclusive?
- Increase access to the general education curriculum?
- Encourage greater participation with peers?

If the answer to any one of these questions was "No," then further discussion and information were needed before making any decision. If the answer was "Yes" across the board, then the idea was immediately given further consideration in terms of next steps, resources, and timelines. The principal reported that these questions gave her clarity, and she shared them with the staff to be more transparent in her decision-making process.

3.5: Review the Vision and Rationale Yearly, Revising as Needed

Once a vision statement has been created, edited, and shared, many leaders say "Phew! There! Done with that!" and expect administrators and staff to actualize it. On the contrary, it is necessary for leaders to provide ongoing support and conduct regular checks to make sure the vision is aligned with day-to-day actions and that educators are held accountable to it. It's easy to slip back into old habits and to allow pressures, new initiatives, or world events to take you off course. Over time, you may find that you need to once again reexamine your vision and rationale to create more inclusive educational opportunities.

One school system we know of holds a recommitment meeting every year to review its vision. Leaders celebrate all their inclusive accomplishments and decide if the vision statement requires any edits. They use this time to reenergize their work, hold one another accountable, discuss how to overcome obstacles, and courageously disrupt any beliefs or practices that do not support their vision.

An inclusive vision statement is often both aspirational *and* action oriented. By nature, it is something that has not yet been achieved, but it uses system data to identify current strengths and inequities and dream for a more inclusive future. Developing a vision and rationale with your leadership team and getting feedback from diverse system members will help establish ownership and understanding of the vision by all. As the leader, it is your responsibility and privilege to both advance and defend the vision. Be prepared to go on the road, stay as long as it takes, and recommit to the vision as often as needed.

Milestone 3: Do we have a clear public vision for inclusion and understanding of the needed system-level changes?
Leadership Questions **Q 3.1** Does the leadership team have a vision for inclusion? **Q 3.2** Does the leadership team have a clear rationale for the shift toward inclusion? **Q 3.3** Has the leadership team included diverse members in the visioning process? **Q 3.4** Is the vision shared publicly? **Q 3.5** Is there a process in place to revisit and revise the vision yearly?
Leadership Steps **S 3.1** Craft or revise a vision statement. **S 3.2** Develop a clear rationale using key findings from your system equity review. **S 3.3** Get feedback on the vision from diverse members of the school system. **S 3.4** Share the finalized vision and rationale widely. **S 3.5** Review the vision and rationale yearly, revising as needed.

Consider your team's discussion around these questions and steps: Where is there clarity and where might your team need to focus additional time and energy? Then, turn to your Action Plan and add any necessary steps.

Your Action Plan

Go to your Action Plan and record any necessary action steps.

4

Realign School Structures to Inclusive Ones

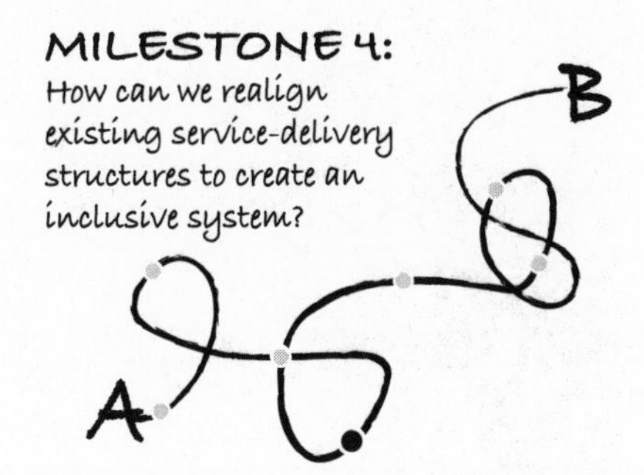

Congratulations, you are at Milestone 4! By now you have a vision for your inclusive system and a rationale that identifies the current structures and practices that are not effectively serving all your students. You have collected and analyzed system data using an equity lens and you have created your system's current service-delivery maps. Now, it is time to align your service delivery with your inclusive vision and address the inequities that your equity review turned up. In this chapter, you'll find examples of ways your leadership team can do this work by looking at the how, when, where, and by whom of service delivery. We show you how other systems have redrawn their service-delivery maps by reallocating staff and creating new inclusive structures for all, and we conclude by discussing how to align IEPs to newly inclusive services and structures and sharing ways to address inevitable issues and obstacles that arise.

4.1: Review Service-Delivery Maps Before and After Inclusive Redesign

In our extensive work with educational leaders, we have found that reviewing before-and-after service-delivery maps from systems that have traveled the path of an inclusive change process is incredibly powerful. It helps leaders see ways to redesign systems so they can make their inclusivity vision a reality. In this section, we walk you through examples of one school system's service-delivery redesign. Before you begin, acquaint yourself with the service-delivery map key shown in Figure 4.1.

Figure 4.1 Service-Delivery Map Key

General Education Teacher	Special Education Teacher	Paraprofessional
■	○	◆

Elementary School Maps

The map in Figure 4.2 shows service delivery before inclusive redesign, when it was composed of 5 special education teachers (circles), 10 paraprofessionals (diamonds), and 21 general education teachers (rectangles). The arrows represent students who were pulled from the general education classroom to receive special education services in special education classrooms (three resource classrooms and one self-contained life skills classroom). The inclusion special education teacher overlaps with a general education teacher to indicate a classroom where the special and general education teachers co-taught. The numbers in the circle indicate that there were 20 students without disabilities and 8 students with disabilities in the co-taught inclusion classroom.

The map in Figure 4.3 shows service delivery at the same school after redesign using only existing staff. There are still 5 special education teachers (circles), 10 paraprofessionals (diamonds), and 21 general education teachers (rectangles). In this map, however, the arrows point from the circles to the rectangles to indicate that the special education teachers are supporting the

Figure 4.2 Sample Elementary School Service-Delivery Map Before Redesign

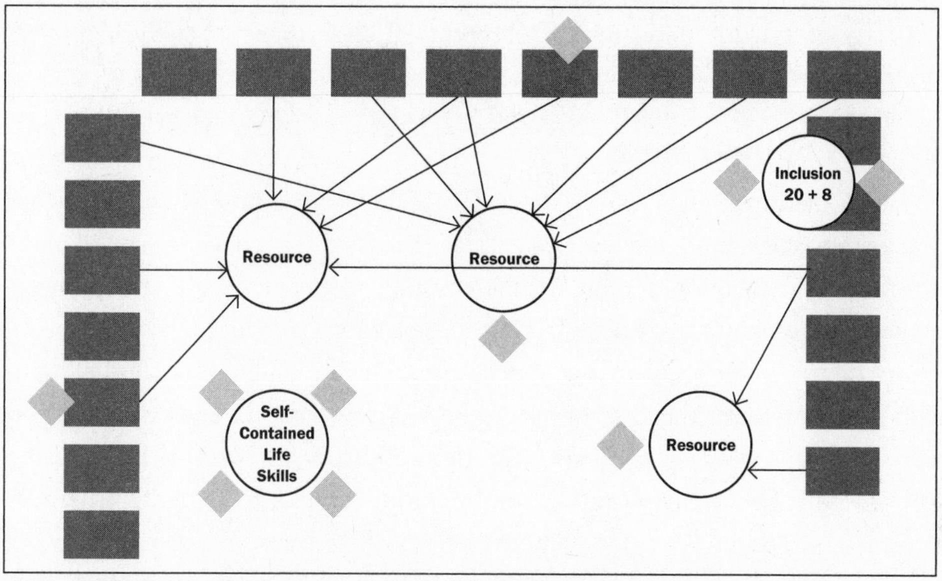

Inclusion
20 + 8
Resource
Resource
Self-
Contained
Life
Skills
Resource

Source: From *Inclusive Reform Service-Delivery Map Examples* by J. Causton & K. MacLeod (2022d), Inclusive Schooling. Copyright 2022 by Inclusive Schooling. Reprinted with permission.

Figure 4.3 Sample Elementary School Service-Delivery Map After Redesign

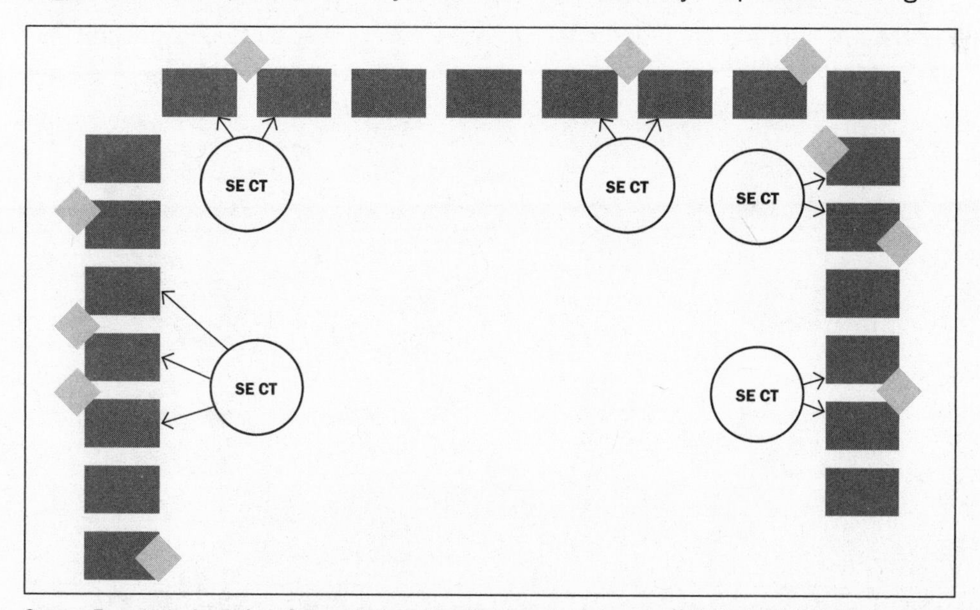

SE CT
SE CT
SE CT
SE CT
SE CT

Source: From *Inclusive Reform Service-Delivery Map Examples* by J. Causton & K. MacLeod (2022d), Inclusive Schooling. Copyright 2022 by Inclusive Schooling. Reprinted with permission.

general education teachers through co-teaching and consulting. The resource rooms and the self-contained life skills room are gone and there is no longer just one co-taught "inclusion" classroom. All classrooms are heterogeneous and inclusive because staff support students in general education.

Middle School Maps

The map in Figure 4.4 shows service delivery in a middle school before inclusivity redesign. There were 21 special education teachers (circles), 15 paraprofessionals (diamonds), and teams of subject-specific grade-level general education teachers (rectangles). The special education teachers are labeled using their specific titles or the special programs in which they worked. Special educators with the title of co-teacher (CT) worked in general education classrooms on grade-level teams. Special educators with the title of tutor/consult delivered a mix of push-in and pull-out services to students on grade-level teams. Special educators who worked in the multiple-handicapped (MH), emotional disability (ED), and cognitive disability (CD) programs were in self-contained classrooms all day. There was one reading specialist who pulled students with IEPs to a separate classroom. Paraprofessionals were largely clustered in the self-contained programs (MH, ED, CD). Two served as 1:1 supports for students in general education classrooms and two served as building float support.

Figure 4.4 Sample Middle School Service-Delivery Map Before Redesign

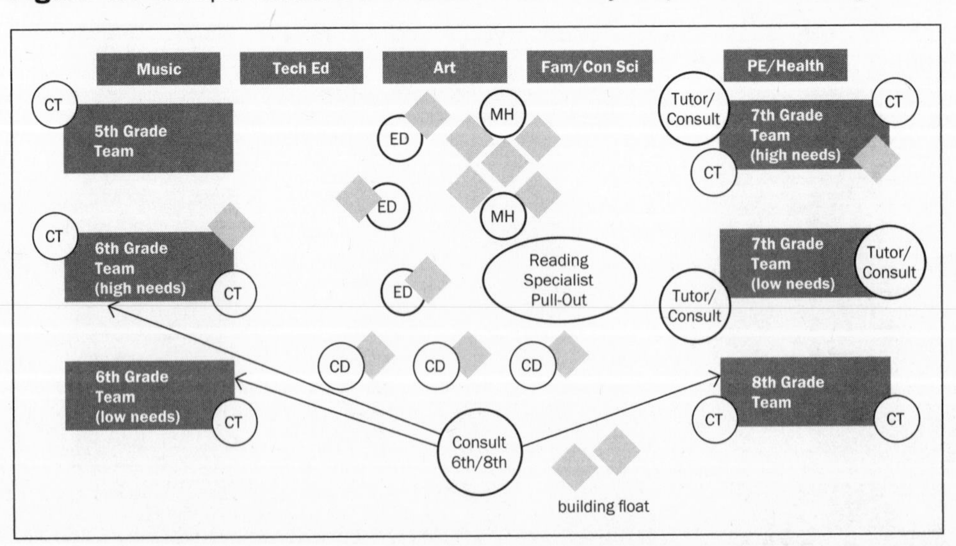

Source: From *Inclusive Reform Service-Delivery Map Examples* by J. Causton & K. MacLeod (2022d), Inclusive Schooling. Copyright 2022 by Inclusive Schooling. Reprinted with permission.

The map in Figure 4.5 shows service delivery in the same school after redesign using only existing staff. There are still 21 special education teachers (circles), 15 paraprofessionals (diamonds), and teams of subject-specific grade-level general education teachers (rectangles). However, special educators no longer work in separate programs, function as pull-out reading specialists, or provide both push-in and pull-out services as consult/tutors. Instead, all special educators now serve as co-teachers or inclusion facilitators. The special education reading specialist now consults to support general education teachers. Most paraprofessionals work as part of inclusive grade-level teams, though two continue to serve as 1:1 supports for students in general education and two float within the building to provide additional student support as needed.

Figure 4.5 Sample Middle School Service-Delivery Map After Redesign

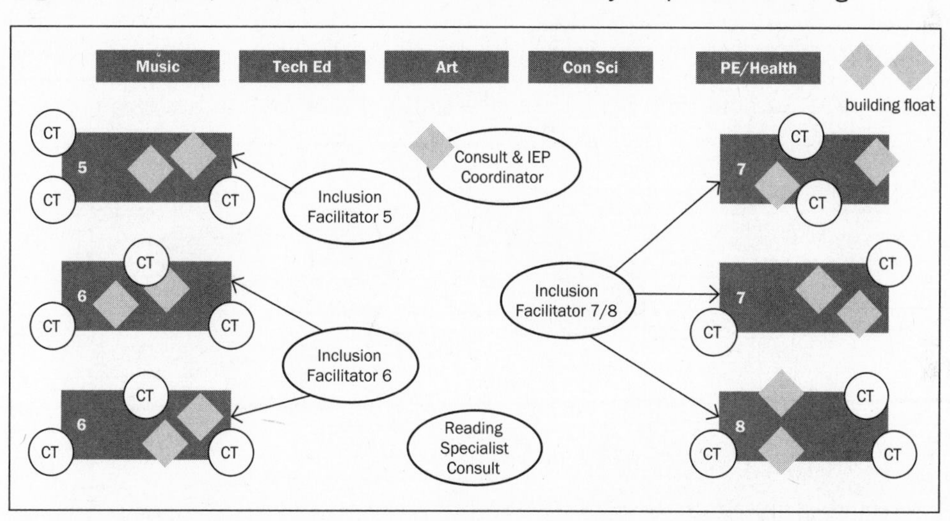

Source: From *Inclusive Reform Service-Delivery Map Examples* by J. Causton & K. MacLeod (2022d), Inclusive Schooling. Copyright 2022 by Inclusive Schooling. Reprinted with permission.

High School Maps

The map in Figure 4.6 (p. 58) shows service delivery at a high school before inclusivity redesign. There were 17 special education teachers (circles), 11 paraprofessionals (diamonds), and teams of subject-specific grade-level general education teachers (rectangles). There were also honors-specific grade-level teams in the 9th and 10th grade. Each special education teacher is labeled with their specific title and/or the special program in which they worked. Many special education teachers had multiple titles and delivered services in multiple settings. For example, Team 1 and Team 2 10th grade special educators co-taught and consulted with general education teachers on those teams and pulled students out to a resource room. Several special educators co-taught on grade-level teams (though only in specific subjects) and pulled students out for resource room services. Two special educators pulled students out for what this system called tutoring—like a resource room but using even smaller groupings of IEP students. Two special educators worked in the self-contained multiple-handicapped (MH) program all day. Two special educators worked in the self-contained alternative education (Alt Ed) program all day. Another special educator served as the career and technical education (CTE) co-teacher and pulled students out for resource and advisory. Paraprofessionals were largely clustered in the self-contained MH and Alt Ed programs and supported students 1:1 in general education.

Figure 4.6 Sample High School Service-Delivery Map Before Redesign

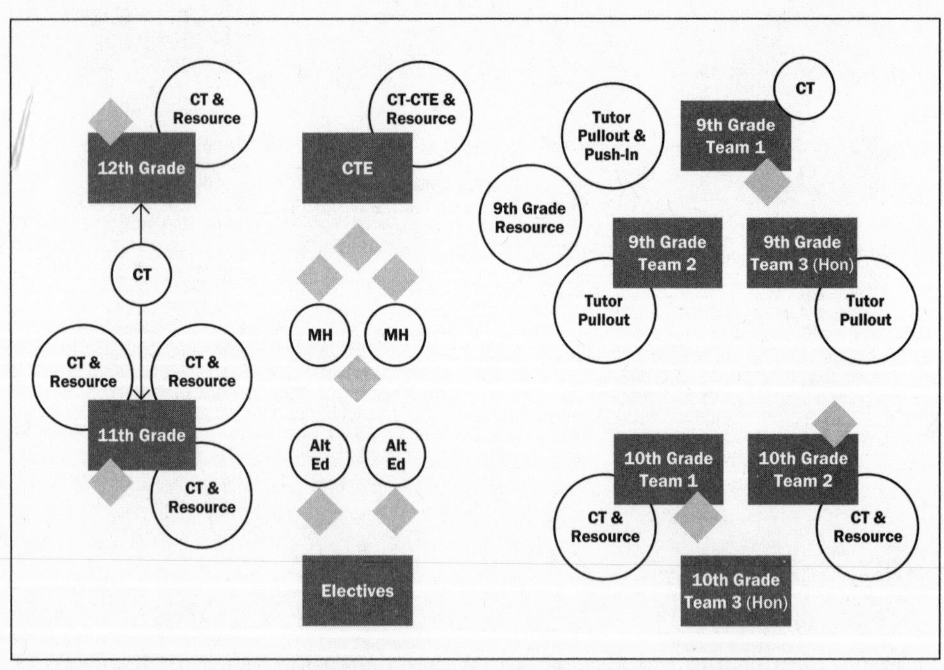

Source: From *Inclusive Reform Service-Delivery Map Examples* by J. Causton & K. MacLeod (2022d), Inclusive Schooling. Copyright 2022 by Inclusive Schooling. Reprinted with permission.

The map in Figure 4.7 shows service delivery at the same high school after redesign using only existing staff. There are still 17 special education teachers (circles), 11 paraprofessionals (diamonds), and teams of subject-specific grade-level general education teachers (rectangles). The leadership team has de-leveled the 9th and 10th grade teams by getting rid of honors-specific teams and ensuring that all teams include heterogeneously grouped students. They also closed the two self-contained MH programs and the separate resource, tutoring, and advisory settings, freeing up those educators to serve as co-teachers and consultants to grade-level teams and electives, or as grade-level inclusion facilitators supporting students with more complex support needs. Paraprofessionals are now dispersed to support grade-level teams, CTE, and specials.

Figure 4.7 Sample High School Service-Delivery Map After Redesign

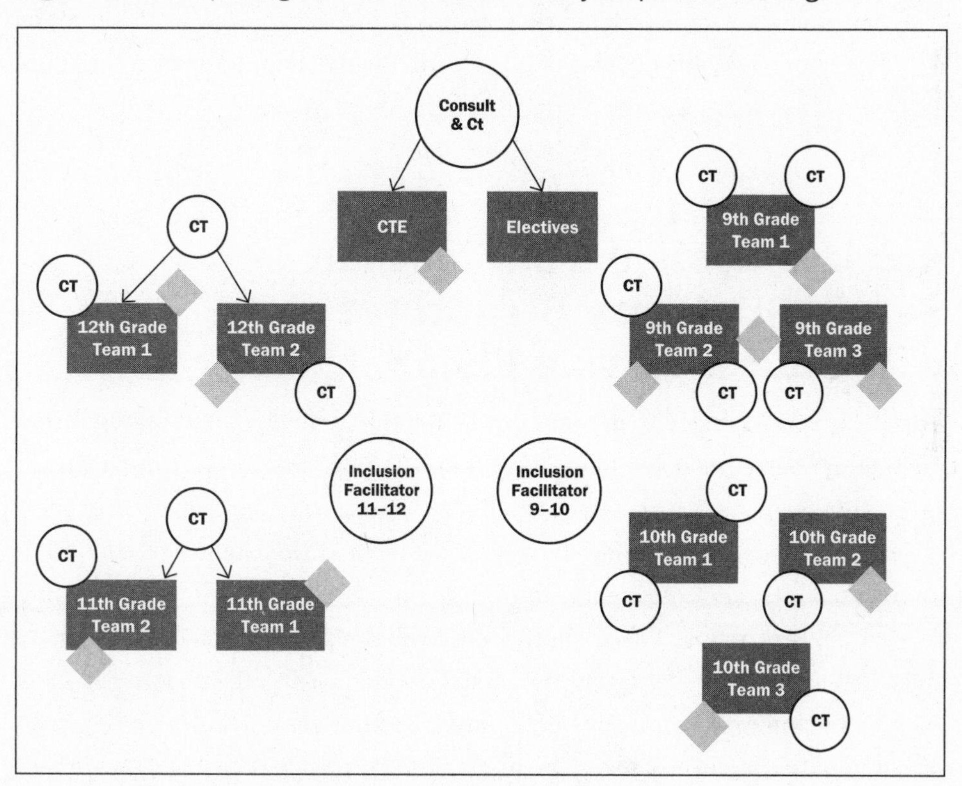

Source: From *Inclusive Reform Service-Delivery Map Examples* by J. Causton & K. MacLeod (2022d), Inclusive Schooling. Copyright 2022 by Inclusive Schooling. Reprinted with permission.

Your leadership team may want to spend time discussing these sample maps before examining your own maps in the next section. Consider the following questions:

- What language or title changes for special educators or programs were made? What might these changes do to the culture of the system?
- In what specific ways did the system expand service-delivery options? Where did they create new options?
- What big questions arise for you when you look at the de-tracking of special education and de-leveling of general education teams across the system?

Loop Ahead: As your leadership team discusses the map redesign examples, you may have questions about scheduling and collaboration. If so, loop ahead to Chapter 5, where we go into detail about inclusive service-delivery options and how to schedule and support personnel in their new roles. Chapter 6 details the types of professional development you will need to help staff learn the skills necessary to take on their new inclusive roles.

4.2: Use System Data to Align Service-Delivery Structures with Your Inclusive Vision

As before, you will need to gather your leadership team and allot enough time for one or more extensive planning sessions to do this work. You will need to examine your current service-delivery maps, consider ways to expand on or create inclusive service-delivery options, and then redesign each map for greater inclusion. To begin, examine your current, building-by-building service-delivery maps. These show your leadership team exactly how many special education teachers, general education teachers, and paraprofessionals each school building or grade level has and how they are currently used to support students and one another. The maps should indicate which staff members pull students from general education classrooms and curriculum, which students learn in separate classrooms, what those separate classrooms and their staff are called, and where paraprofessionals are being utilized (or underutilized). Depending on the system, you may wish to include additional personnel in your maps such as related service providers, Title 1 teachers, or teachers of multilingual learners.

Loop Back: In Chapter 2, we took you through how to collect specific system data and use it to create service-delivery maps. If your team hasn't done so yet, you will want to loop back and create those maps so that you can use them to redesign for more inclusive service delivery.

As your team reviews the service-delivery maps, consider the following questions:

- How can we redesign services so that all staff serve all students inclusively?
- How can we redesign services so that specific classrooms are not overcrowded with paraprofessionals or other adults?
- How can we redesign services so that specific classrooms are not supporting and educating a disproportionate number of students with IEPs?
- Is it possible to redesign services by shifting staff roles rather than hiring additional staff?

The answers to these questions will help guide your team as you redesign your service-delivery maps—a huge and exciting step, so congratulations! Your redesign will help your system address existing inequities for students and more closely align with federal law and research.

4.3: Align IEPs with New Inclusive Structures

Your next step is to ensure your students' IEPs reflect the redesign. You will need to communicate the shift from placements to services to families and get clarity on how to write inclusive service delivery into IEPs. Of course, this also means addressing big questions that staff and families will have to ensure the IEP process supports each student individually and moves your inclusive vision forward.

Communicate with Families

Rather than asking case managers to explain new service delivery at student IEP meetings, we recommend system leaders do this work themselves.

Flipping the Script

By a director of special education

When seeking to move toward a more inclusive model, our team realized that families might find our rationale for change confusing. Many families had been told for years that their children required separate, specialized placements, and they suddenly felt as though we were "flipping the script" on them by taking the opposite stance.

Our administrative team took responsibility for reaching out to families instead of case managers for a couple of key reasons. First, inclusive education was a new concept to our staff, and not all of them embraced it. Our administrative team shared the vision for inclusion and how it would be executed. To aid in the conversations, I provided talking points to our building principals and special education administrators to address questions that might arise, ensuring that we were all delivering a similar message to families. The second reason our leaders assumed responsibility for these discussions is related to trust: We needed to strike a delicate balance between communicating the rationale behind inclusion and supporting the relationships between families and a system that had previously segregated their children.

I am happy to report that this part of our plan went very well, and we had minimal concerns from families of students with IEPs. This was remarkable given that we were serving a system that educated roughly 2,200 students with disabilities in placements that were previously largely restrictive. Without leaders willing to engage in challenging conversations and consistency in our beliefs and messages, our efforts might have been thwarted.

Common Obstacles Related to the IEP

Even if your leadership team has expertly communicated with families and staff about your shift toward inclusive service delivery, some community members may still raise concerns connected to the IEP. In this section, we present the most commonly raised concerns and respond with clear rationales related to the IEP and the law.

"But the IEP Says..."

When moving from placements to services, it is common for staff to suggest that proposed changes are in conflict with IEPs. The fact is, an IEP is a flexible document that can and should be revised as often as necessary by IEP team members. It is developed by teams to ensure a student's access, participation, and progress in the general curriculum. IDEA encourages reviewing and revising IEPs whenever needed to ensure that students are getting appropriate services and supports and making progress toward their goals within general education (Section 300.320[a][2]). IDEA also states that "changes to the IEP may be made either by the entire IEP team at an IEP team meeting, or... by amending the IEP rather than by redrafting the entire IEP. Upon request, a parent must be provided with a revised copy of the IEP with the amendments incorporated" (Section 300.324). Ensuring your staff hear about the flexibility of the IEP and the legal preference for inclusion again and again from leaders at both the building and the central-office level is very important.

"But This Student Needs a Resource Room"

No room—not even a resource room—is a service in and of itself. Services are portable and brought to students, and those included in an IEP should support the student's access to general education and their inclusion in the school community. Once an IEP team has determined the individual strengths and needs of the student, it should outline how to provide appropriate services inclusively, whether that means access to a co-taught classroom to support needs in reading and writing or material accommodations to support executive functioning skills throughout the day.

Loop Back: If you want to review the clear legal preference for portable services, loop back to Figure 1.2 (p. 21) in Chapter 1 and review the Roncker v. Walter (1983) case.

"But We Need to Deliver Specially Designed Instruction"

Leaders often get questions about how teachers can provide specially designed instruction (SDI) and accompanying support minutes in the general education classroom without students participating in something separate or alternate. IDEA states that SDI means adapting, as appropriate to the needs of an eligible child, the content, methodology, or delivery of instruction (Section 300.39). When this concern is raised, help team members understand that SDI is simply a way to help ensure that an individual student receives access to the general education curriculum and setting; therefore, the best place to provide SDI is embedded into the general education curriculum and classroom.

"But We Need a Continuum of Placements"

We sometimes hear that separate placements and programs need to exist because of the continuum of alternative placement for services, which is part of the LRE principle of IDEA. Unfortunately, this principle is largely misunderstood and leads to an overreliance on restrictive placement and programs. If they take a deeper look at the LRE principle of IDEA, leaders will find it does not reference a setting. The principle is more about the decisions made by the IEP team in terms of services and supports and where and how those can be best provided. What's more, when referencing services and supports, IDEA defines supplementary aids and services to mean "aids, services, and other supports that are provided in regular education classes, other education-related settings, and in extracurricular and nonacademic settings, to enable children with disabilities to be educated with nondisabled children to the maximum extent appropriate" (Section 300.42). This means we must exhaust all supplementary aids and services before even considering a placement in a more restrictive setting.

Further, IDEA does not require a school system to have each possible placement option along the continuum *filled* with students; it only requires that the system make the option available *if needed*. Decades of research and special education case law all confirm that inclusion in general education is better for students. Leaders can commit to creating school systems designed to benefit all students while still providing appropriate inclusive supports to students with disabilities. As leaders, we can and must do better than rely on the myth of the LRE continuum to justify separate placements.

"But Isn't Placement an Individual Team Decision?"

Yes! And again, special education services, not separate placements and programs, begin with thoughtful consideration of the individual student's needs at the IEP meeting. IEPs are written to provide students with access to general education content, curriculum, and peers. IDEA requires that "children with disabilities... are educated with children who are nondisabled; and special classes, separate schooling, or other removal... occurs only if the nature or severity of the disability is such that education in regular classes with the use of supplementary aids and services cannot be achieved satisfactorily" (IDEA Section 1412 [a] [5], 2004).

Despite the high standard for removal and preference for general education stated in IDEA, teams often assume that participation in the regular classroom is not possible or that a student needs to start off in a segregated space to learn skills before they are allowed to access, participate in, and progress in the general curriculum. We invite you and your leadership team to start with the assumption that services and supports can be provided in the general curriculum for all students with an IEP and then to truly consider a whole variety of actions before removing the student. When making individual decisions, the team should engage in meaningful conversations centered around the following questions:

- Are there creative service-delivery or scheduling options we could adopt to ensure the student remains in general education?
- What challenges do we foresee with the student participating in general education, and what are some potential strategies to overcome them?
- What systemwide barriers exist that lead us to believe a separate or segregated setting is best for students?

When considering these questions in tandem with the law, it becomes apparent that there are many potential ways to include a student in general education. Rather than assuming removal is the only way to meet the needs arising from a child's disability, really dig into these conversations to determine the supplementary aids and services that can be provided inclusively.

"Are There Exceptions to Inclusion?"

This is a common question we get asked. After considering the research and legal preference for inclusive education, identifying inequities in your own system data, exploring all possible inclusive service-delivery options, committing to creative and flexible options to support all students, bringing all possible supplementary aids and services to the student, and collecting data on the use of all supports, then—and only then—do we recommend a very short-term placement in a separate and more restrictive setting. Some students may require temporary hospital or home education to support serious mental health needs. Regardless, there should always be a clear and urgent plan in place to return the student to the general education setting.

Though daunting, realigning your system to create more inclusive service delivery for all students is one of the most exciting steps in the inclusive change process. When your leadership team gathers to consider your current service-delivery maps and realign them for greater inclusion, you can guide the work knowing you are redrawing your maps to develop a system that truly maximizes your resources to provide the most inclusive, efficient, and appropriate support for every single student in your system.

Milestone 4: How can we realign existing service-delivery structures to create an inclusive system?
Leadership Questions **Q 4.1** Where are our service-delivery structures out of alignment with our inclusive vision? **Q 4.2** How do we better align service-delivery structures with our inclusive vision? **Q 4.3** How do we use the IEP as a vehicle for effective inclusive change? **Leadership Steps** **S 4.1** Review service-delivery maps before and after inclusive redesign. **S 4.2** Use system data to align service-delivery structures with your inclusive vision. **S 4.3** Align IEPs with new inclusive structures.

Consider your team's discussion around these questions and steps: Where is there clarity and where might your team need to focus additional time and energy? Then, turn to your Action Plan and add any necessary steps.

Your Action Plan

Go to your Action Plan and record any necessary action steps.

5

Reimagine the Schedule and Collaborative Staff Roles

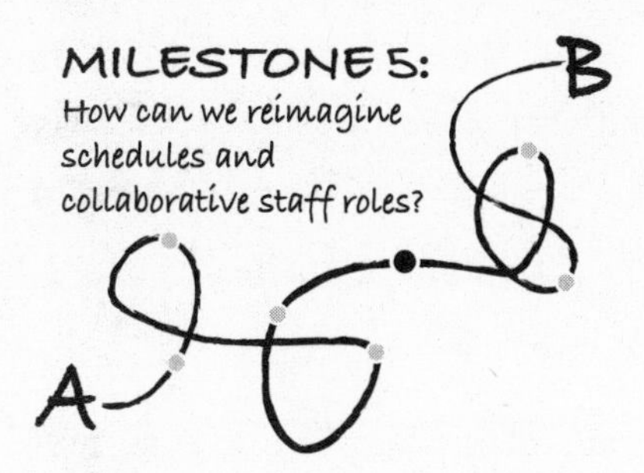

Congratulations on reaching Milestone 5! You are moving forward to redesign your system. As you shift from separate placements and programs to inclusive service delivery, not only does the system begin to better meet the needs of all students, but you get to reimagine the ways in which educators and support staff work and teach together. Leaders will quickly learn that collaboration and co-planning are the real magic behind effective inclusive school systems. Educators, specialists, and support staff must work together in highly coordinated ways to give all students seamless differentiated access to general education curriculum and provide academic and social support to students with and without disabilities.

In this chapter, we focus on ways leaders can use the schedule to support realigned service delivery using new inclusive staff roles. We first share collaborative and inclusive service-delivery options to help you explore possibilities. Next, we share our stepwise Inclusive System Scheduling Process (Causton et al., 2022b). Then, we share ways to carve out time in the schedule for collaborative planning. We provide you with the details and tools you will need to best support your staff to collaborate effectively *and* strategically. We also share innovative ways leaders have addressed challenges or obstacles around scheduling and new collaborative roles.

5.1: Learn About Collaborative Roles and Inclusive Service Delivery

To better understand how moving toward a new inclusive system may impact service delivery, language, roles, and responsibilities for staff, review the Collaborative and Inclusive Service Delivery Roles and Tips (Causton et al., 2022c) document in Figure 5.1. In this table, we outline how staff might provide a variety of inclusive service-delivery options and how those options may impact collaborative roles. We also share helpful implementation tips. The collaborative roles and responsibilities your inclusive staff will take on are much broader than what we highlight here, but you can use this information as a starting place to explore possibilities for your inclusive system.

Loop Ahead: Visit Chapter 6 to read more about how to support your staff with effective professional development as they take on new collaborative roles and responsibilities.

More Is Not Always More

By a special education administrator

I was chairing the IEP team for a 5th grade student who was struggling with organization skills and found that I needed to challenge the thinking of some team members. Several teachers lamented that the student "needs help getting materials ready and paying attention," and that he "doesn't do anything on his own." The team also felt strongly that the student needed a 1:1 paraprofessional to be successful.

Figure 5.1 Collaborative and Inclusive Service Delivery Roles and Tips

Position	Service-Delivery Option	Collaborative Roles	Implementation Tips
General Educator	**Co-Teacher**	• Collaborates with inclusive staff teams to develop curriculum that meets the needs of all learners • Provides instruction for all students in the general education classroom • Co-teaches with a general education teacher or inclusive staff member for some part of the day—whether a single class block or period, all day long, or somewhere in between	• Ensure that general education teachers understand how they can co-teach with special educators, related service providers, and paraprofessionals. • Provide planning time, professional development, and ongoing coaching to help general educators intentionally use effective co-teaching models (e.g., station teaching, one-teach/one-make multisensory instruction). • Help co-teachers to differentiate lessons for students with significant support needs and those who need greater challenges.
Special Educator	**Co-Teacher**	Co-teaches with a general education teacher for some part of the day—whether a single class block or period, all day long, or somewhere in between	• Strategically support key areas/subjects and student needs. • Provide planning time, professional development, and ongoing coaching to help special educators intentionally use effective co-teaching models (e.g., station teaching, one-teach/one-make multisensory instruction).
	Consultative Support	• Provides in-class support on a regularly scheduled basis; support may occur daily, but frequency is flexible • Provides behind-the-scenes lesson planning, coaching, and modifying or adapting content and materials	• Provide strategic in-class supports for key subjects/areas of need. • Support grade-level teams and students with lower-level support needs. • Provide planning time, professional development, and ongoing coaching to help special educators to effectively consult with other educators (e.g., to engage in role release and role extension).

(continued)

Figure 5.1 Collaborative and Inclusive Service Delivery Roles and Tips—(*continued*)

Position	Service-Delivery Option	Collaborative Roles	Implementation Tips
Special Educator—(*continued*)	**Inclusion Facilitator**	• Coordinates services for students with significant disabilities in general education classrooms • Works behind the scenes to provide ongoing coaching and job-embedded professional development to teachers, paraprofessionals, and related service providers on inclusive practices • Serves as a resource and support for creating modifications and accommodations, providing behavioral suggestions, and ensuring that service delivery is coordinated	• Relinquish responsibilities for instruction to maintain a flexible schedule that enables attendance at grade-level or department planning meetings, classroom support for job-embedded coaching, and making student-specific accommodations and modifications. • Provide planning time, professional development, and ongoing coaching to help inclusion facilitators design and deliver job-embedded support for educators, paraprofessionals, and related service providers.
Related Services (OT, PT, SLP, Orientation and Mobility Specialist, Vision Specialist, etc.)	**In-Class Consultant**	• Provides students on their caseload with interventions that are embedded into general education lessons and activities • Provides grade-level or building-level training and support to meet the needs of many students in inclusive settings • Collaborates with other staff, exchanges information, and teaches other team members how to meet a range of learner needs	• To avoid scheduling obstacles and increase flexibility, recommend a schedule of in-class support for caseload students (e.g., four times monthly, six times quarterly). • Caseloads can be assigned based on student groupings in specific general education classes or teams. • Provide planning time, professional development, and ongoing coaching to help related service providers embed interventions into general education lessons and activities, support grade-level and building-level teams, and collaborate effectively across disciplines.
Paraprofessional	**Classroom or Team/Grade-Level Support**	• Provides "just in time" support to all students in general education classes	• Ensure that paraprofessionals understand how they can co-teach under the supervision of general and/or special educators and related service providers.

Position	Service-Delivery Option	Collaborative Roles	Implementation Tips
Para-professional —*(continued)*	**Classroom or Team/Grade-Level Support —*(continued)***	• Collaborates with classroom, team-based, or grade-level staff to follow and help implement lesson plans and deliver specially designed instruction related to students' IEPs • Provides input on student support and instruction	• Provide planning time, professional development, and ongoing coaching to help paraprofessionals effectively co-teach and provide support to all students across differentiated lessons.
	1:1 Support	In addition to the roles listed above, provides individualized support to a particular student, working with inclusive staff to fade 1:1 support whenever possible	• Should be assigned sparingly and material and instructional supplementary supports should be offered beforehand. • Provide planning time, professional development, and ongoing coaching to help ensure 1:1 paraprofessionals are highly trained in providing natural and seamless support and work with their team to fade support.

Source: From *Collaborative and Inclusive Service Delivery* by J. Causton, K. MacLeod, & K. Pretti-Frontczak, 2022, Inclusive Schooling. Copyright 2022 by Inclusive Schooling. Reprinted with permission.

I left the meeting feeling like I needed to find a way to help the team think differently about the student and his support needs. At our next meeting, I started by asking the team to think of the student's strengths and find times when he was pretty organized and able to work independently. We found numerous situations where this young man initiated tasks and completed work, particularly when he was engaged and interested in the topic. Next, I asked the team to describe the ways a paraprofessional would help meet the student's goals around organization and independence. One teacher replied that the paraprofessional would help the student retrieve his materials, stay on task, and write down his homework. I asked the team to think about the root cause behind the student's lack of engagement, follow-through, and independence. I then encouraged my team to see that, rather than hiring support personnel, we could find ways to increase his engagement during instructional tasks and explicitly teach him the skills required to organize his materials and write down his homework.

The bottom line is that more staff is not always the answer, and in fact can be detrimental to student progress when it is not carefully considered. The addition of a paraprofessional in this instance would serve as merely a Band-Aid on the true problem. Although an additional staff member may have temporarily helped the student make sure his materials were out and his homework was written down, the student would not learn how to perform these tasks independently.

5.2: Identify Ways to Strategically and Flexibly Schedule Staff to Serve All Students Inclusively

A schedule essentially tells us how we use our staff, space, and time. It reflects the values and priorities of those who work within it. If we look at a master school system schedule, we can easily see what the system values. For example, if we have several staffed resource rooms, then we are valuing pull-out instruction. If we assign several special education teachers and paraprofessionals to staff a life-skills class, then our values prioritize a medical model of disability focused on removing and remediating deficits in separate spaces and with separate curriculum. If, instead, students with disabilities are receiving services in general education classrooms with grade-level peers, then we are living our vision and values of ensuring inclusive education for all.

Often, leaders inherit the schedules and scheduling decisions—and the values these represent—of those who previously worked in the system. The great news for your inclusive journey is that you can redesign the schedule to strategically use staff in ways that align with your inclusive vision and create a more seamless and collaborative support system for each student. In this section, we guide you through the Inclusive System Scheduling Process in Figure 5.2 (and in Appendix E, p. 121) to help you masterfully schedule using your existing staff in collaborative and flexible ways.

The Inclusive System Scheduling Process

Now that you have your service-delivery maps for each building, understand how many staff members and sections are available, and have reviewed inclusive service-delivery possibilities, it is time to assign students to general education classrooms and reassign staff to collaboratively and inclusively provide support. This system-level scheduling process, done in a specific order,

Figure 5.2 Inclusive System Scheduling Process

Phase 1: Schedule Students into General Education Classrooms	
Step ①:	Start by scheduling students with significant support needs into classrooms. Make sure they are spread across general education classrooms and not clustered, using natural proportions as your guide.
Step ②:	Next, consider all students' support needs. **Step 2a: Consider levels of support.** Inclusion facilitators might support students with more significant needs, co-teachers might support students with medium to high support needs, and consultative services might support students with low to medium needs. **Step 2b: Consider cross-categorical support.** In a cross-categorical approach, special education teachers support all students with IEPs regardless of disability label or level of need. Leaders can divide up teacher caseloads equally or in a way that makes sense for educator workload using flexible roles to meet the needs of students.
Step ③:	Create balanced and diverse general education classes by placing students with a range of academic, behavioral, and social-emotional needs across classes.
Step ④:	Strategically assign students to general education classrooms so they have access to the necessary staff and levels of support (e.g., co-teachers, consultative services, inclusion facilitators).
Step ⑤:	Assign groups of students to specific general education classes based on related service needs.
Step ⑥:	Strategically place students in general education classes who do not have disability labels but have other significant needs, being careful not to create classes that have high percentages of students with significant needs.
Step ⑦:	Assign all other students without disability labels heterogeneously to general education classrooms.
Phase 2: Schedule Educators and Related Service Providers	
Step ①:	Review how many members of your potential staff there are: special educators, related service providers, gifted and talented educators, educators of multilingual learners, Title 1 educators, reading specialists, coaches, and so on.
Step ②:	Assign staff based on inclusive support structures and student needs (e.g., co-teachers, consultative services, inclusion facilitators), not labels.
Step ③:	Assign staff to classes and to students considering both caseloads and workloads.
Step ④:	Reduce the number of different classrooms that a single educator or related service provider supports.
Step ⑤:	Reduce the number of buildings and classrooms that educators and related service providers support.
Step ⑥:	Create common and meaningful planning time by aligning preparation or planning periods.
Phase 3: Schedule Paraprofessionals	
Step ①:	Assign paraprofessionals to classrooms, grade levels, groups of students, or even an entire building as floaters to support students and educators as needed.
Step ②:	For students assigned a 1:1 paraprofessional, determine if the 1:1 support is still necessary in a new inclusive system.

Source: From *The Inclusive System Scheduling Process* by J. Causton, K. MacLeod, & K. Pretti-Frontczak, 2022, Inclusive Schooling. Copyright 2022 by Inclusive Schooling. Reprinted with permission.

will ensure that you prioritize the inclusion of students with disabilities, create collaborative schedules for staff, and set everyone up for success. In short, masterful scheduling can help you turn your inclusive vision into reality. We suggest using the phases described in Figure 5.2 and adapting as needed.

We know that a single decision can cause a cascade of new issues when creating an inclusive schedule for students and staff. As you address each issue, we encourage you to consistently return to your inclusive vision, priorities, and dreams and then remember that many have traveled this path before. In Figure 5.3, we share some of our most effective scheduling tips.

Figure 5.3 Scheduling Implementation Tips

Use a collaborative space or document to draft the schedule.	Using a common or shared document allows everyone to review the factors that are guiding decisions, ensure everyone is aware of critical moving parts, and be meaningfully involved in finding solutions.
Create a working definition of key terms.	Be clear about all relevant terms. Does everyone understand and share common definitions of *significant support needs*, *natural proportions*, *caseload*, *workload*, *inclusion facilitator*, and so on?
Address both caseload and workload.	Analyze students' needs to create strategic caseloads that provide equitable workloads for staff. For example, the inclusion facilitator supporting students with the most complex support needs in a middle school may have fewer students on their caseload than the special educator who co-teaches and consults with the inclusive 6th grade team.
Schedule a universal support block.	• Create an additional block of time in the schedule that is available for *all* students to receive intervention or enrichment. Any student can receive targeted support based on needs. The intervention and enrichment block is a supplement to core instruction, not a replacement (Rufo & Causton, 2022). • All available staff should be used during this block and assigned based on student needs.
Consider requirements based on system size.	For large systems: • Central office staff should provide buildings with guiding principles for scheduling, recognizing that while each building has a unique culture and features, they all act with the same values in mind. • Break larger system-level schedules down into small, manageable parts (e.g., by building, by teams). • Determine where consistency is needed across the system. For small systems: • A small staff can still be flexible, strategic, and creatively inclusive. When scheduling support for student needs in general education, use all available staff. • Leaders can also focus on helping general education staff to become dual-certified and/or paraprofessionals to earn special education teacher certification.

An Inclusive Schedule

By an elementary school principal

One of the concerns that arises when developing an inclusive master schedule is how to ensure that students receive the specialized services they need while continuing to receive access to the general curriculum. We combated this problem with a two-pronged approach.

First, we intentionally structured general education class periods to ensure that research-based best practices were reflected in our instruction. For example, by allocating instructional minutes in the literacy block to align with evidence-based reading instruction, we were able to better ensure that students were receiving strong Tier 1 instruction. This also enabled us to provide in-class support from special educators, paraprofessionals, or instructional specialists at key times to maximize the available resources.

Second, we developed an intervention and enrichment block as part of the master schedule. This was a time when any student could receive strategic support or extension supports. By prioritizing this block in the schedule, we were able to maintain the integrity of the general curriculum and provide additional support and extensions in ways that didn't require any student to be tracked or to miss instruction to receive interventions and enrichments.

5.3: Carve Out Time in the Schedule for Staff to Collaboratively Plan and Provide Ongoing Support

A leadership priority when helping staff adopt new inclusive roles and responsibilities is to ensure they have not only time to meet and plan together, but also ongoing support. Collaborative planning time provides team members with the opportunity to learn about one another and their expertise, understand their new shared roles and responsibilities, and strategically co-develop curriculum, instruction, and individual student supports to best meet the needs of their diverse students. Research and our experiences have repeatedly shown that when leaders provide sacred time for co-planning, staff experience significant professional growth (Hackett et al., 2021; Scruggs et al., 2007) and classroom instruction for all students improves (Hunter et al., 2014). Providing ongoing support for this commitment to planning time means you will need to help staff use their time effectively and make sure that they do not get pulled for other duties during planning time.

A system-level schedule that embeds collaborative planning time for inclusive teams is our best implementation tip. We suggest providing teams with one or two planning blocks per week. For example, you can create grade-level teams of general and special educators, paraprofessionals, and other specialists and assign the team co-planning time directly in the schedule.

To further support planning time, empower staff to be part of the process. Get input directly from teams. Ask them how much planning time they need and when they would prefer it given all their other responsibilities. Help them to understand that while their needs and preferences will be considered, they will be balanced against the needs and preferences of all teams in the school.

Creative Ideas for More Collaborative Planning Time

Great inclusive leaders do everything they can to make sure staff have the necessary planning time. This means taking everything into consideration, from budget to time-bending. The following ideas have worked for many leaders, though of course we encourage you to keep brainstorming as needed.

- **Eliminate duties.** Reconsider duties (e.g., lunchroom support, hall monitoring, bus duty) for anyone with a substantial collaboration and co-planning expectation. Instead of sharing in these traditional duties, these individuals spend more time co-planning.
- **Time-bend.** Help staff use time most efficiently:
  - Use a quick-minute problem-solving process. Set up the problem quickly, and then set a timer for three to five minutes of brainstorming. Make a decision and move on.
  - Use efficient and effective meeting strategies and tools: lesson planning formats, meeting agendas, role cards, timers, action steps, to-do lists.
- **Compensate time.** If the 3rd grade team wants to plan monthly on a Thursday from 4:00 to 7:30 p.m., compensate them for their time.
- **Purchase time.** Whenever possible, use monthly subs and pay teams for half-day, full-day, and even summertime planning sessions. Use a rotating set of subs to create regular co-planning time for teams.
- **Repurpose time.** Use assemblies, arrival, electives or specials, and dismissal time to plan. Ask teachers to get strategic. For example, if students

are at an assembly, get someone else to supervise so the team is freed up to meet and plan.

- **Avoid certain times.** Avoid lunch and other nonpaid time for co-planning periods. If people choose to plan outside the contract day (which many people do), just be sure that the expectation is not for it to happen during nonpaid time.
- **Plan asynchronously.** Use shared electronic documents to create, edit, comment, chat, and keep track of ideas together. For example, the general education teacher inputs the objective for the lesson and some lesson steps, the special education teacher comes in and adds ideas for differentiating the lesson, and then the paraprofessional accesses the document to familiarize themselves and ask questions related to particular students' needs. Communication continues via text messages, email, or apps like Slack or Marco Polo.

Prioritizing inclusive practices through intentional scheduling and common planning time is essential to the growth and success of an inclusive school system. The Inclusive System Scheduling Process should help you make clear, step-by-step decisions as you go. Understanding student support needs and flexible service-delivery models is key to building new infrastructures that reimagine special education in more productive and inclusive ways.

Milestone 5: How can we reimagine schedules and collaborative staff roles?
Leadership Questions **Q 5.1** How can the leadership team strategically and flexibly schedule existing staff? **Q 5.2** How will the leadership team explore and communicate the reimagined collaborative roles and responsibilities for new inclusive service delivery? **Q 5.3** How will the leadership team ensure and support collaborative instructional planning time? **Leadership Steps** **S 5.1** Learn about collaborative roles and inclusive service delivery. **S 5.2** Identify ways to strategically and flexibly schedule staff to serve all students inclusively. **S 5.3** Carve out time in the schedule for staff to collaboratively plan and provide ongoing support.

Consider your team's discussion around these questions and steps: Where is there clarity and where might your team need to focus additional time and energy? Then, turn to your Action Plan and add any necessary steps.

Your Action Plan

Go to your Action Plan and record any necessary action steps.

6

Use Powerful Inclusive Classroom Practices

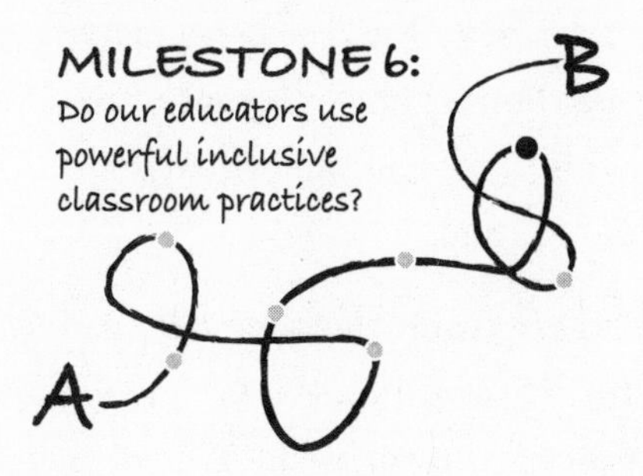

Congratulations! You are now at Milestone 6 and diving deep into the powerful classroom practices that help an inclusive system to thrive. As you move to an inclusive and collaborative service-delivery model, and as you collapse separate placements and programs for students with IEPs, common questions will arise, including "How will I reach and teach each of my students?" "How will I meet all their academic and behavioral needs?" and "How will my staff take on new roles and responsibilities?" Great leaders address staff questions and concerns by identifying areas of success and areas of growth within the system related to classroom practices, developing a robust professional development plan grounded in effective adult learning principles, and supporting staff as they adopt and get feedback on the implementation of new learning and inclusive classroom practices.

In this chapter, we describe five powerful inclusive classroom practices. We explain how leaders can create a systematic professional development plan using the system data collected in Chapter 2, then highlight common professional learning needs and share the essentials of effective professional development (PD). We provide ways to further support staff learning and growth from PLCs to coaching, and finally we share how to set expectations and provide meaningful feedback and evaluate your PD plan to be sure everyone is learning and growing.

6.1: Explore Highly Effective Inclusive Classroom Practices and Identify Growth Opportunities

More than five decades of research and our extensive experience supporting inclusive system change point to five powerful classroom practices. As leaders and educators learn about and adopt these inclusive practices, they may need to unlearn and explore old mindsets and ways of teaching and addressing IEP goals. But this worthwhile and courageous work will set the foundation for inclusive success in your system.

1. **Collaborate and co-teach to reach all students.** Inclusive education requires educators to work together to teach a wide range of learners. Sometimes this occurs in the form of a co-teaching relationship, other times through consultative support. Regardless, any time multiple adults are responsible for the teaching and learning of a diverse group of students, effective co-teaching practices need to be utilized. The well-documented benefits of co-teaching include reducing the student-to-teacher ratio and increasing responsiveness to students (Kuntz & Carter, 2021; Scruggs et al., 2007), creating more access points to learning (Hackett et al., 2021), and making learning more novel and fun. In excellent co-taught classrooms, all staff share instructional planning responsibilities, instructional duties, and ownership for student outcomes. Co-teaching can be accomplished using several different models, including station teaching, one-teach/one-make multisensory instruction, and parallel teaching (described in depth in Appendix F, p. 122), and creates flexible, heterogeneous groupings in which students feel more supported (McDuffie et al., 2009).

2. **Plan universally designed and differentiated instruction.** To reach all students in the general education classroom, core instruction must address a wide range of learners. This means staff collaborate to design instruction that provides students with multiple ways to access content, process information, and show what they've learned. Designing this type of engaging universally designed and differentiated instruction means staff will use student strengths, needs, and cultural and personal identities to plan instruction that is tailored to a uniquely wonderful and diverse class. When this type of instruction occurs across all general education classrooms, students no longer need to leave to receive interventions or supports (McCart & Miller, 2019). Students will not only have greater access to grade-level content but also be better engaged with instruction that reflects their identities, supports their needs, engages their motivation, and celebrates their strengths. Designing instruction in this manner communicates that diversity is valued and celebrated by a system.
3. **Create adaptations to support access to grade-level content.** Though engaging and differentiated core instruction significantly supports students with IEPs, further adaptations such as accommodations and modifications will be needed to give students greater access to general education content and standards. Within an inclusive school system that implements collaboration and differentiated instruction, creating adaptations for specific students will feel like a natural extension of this work. Students and staff will become accustomed to the variety of ways students can access grade-level content and participate in classroom activities. By identifying individual students' needs, prioritizing skills and goals, and developing adaptations, we can meaningfully include students in the general education classroom (Kurth & Keegan, 2014) and make progress in grade-level curriculum (Lee et al., 2010).
4. **Prioritize natural supports.** The term *natural supports* refers to the network of existing supports available to an individual. This could be in the form of systemic supports and resources available to all students using the concept of universally designed instruction, or in the form of peers and community members. To provide students with meaningful access to the curriculum, it is critical to give them opportunities to utilize their network of natural supports so they can increase their independence, autonomy, and sense of belonging. For example, staff in

inclusive systems know how to provide universally designed instruction that offers multiple access points with limited or no support from the start for content and activities to increase independence. Inclusive staff also know how to facilitate peer support that increases interdependence (Brock et al., 2016; Causton-Theoharis & Malmgren, 2005). Excessive support from staff can be a significant barrier to student success (Cameron, 2014; Giangreco et al., 2010), so all staff should work together to plan for a focus on increased natural supports and intentionally work to fade 1:1 adult support whenever possible.

5. **Provide inclusive behavior supports.** Even when very talented educators leverage the full power of the four inclusive classroom practices mentioned so far, additional support to help students who display challenging behaviors will sometimes be needed. Students with emotional and behavioral support needs or labels are among the most segregated populations of students and more likely than their peers with other disability labels to drop out of school (U.S. Department of Education, 2020); they are also at highest risk for punishment and disciplinary action (National Longitudinal Transition Study-2, 2006). In inclusive systems, educators understand the communicative role of challenging behavior and the science of behavior (e.g., stress leads directly to reactive behavior) and commit to learning how to reduce stressors for students. All staff possess a deep toolbox for providing students with consistent, compassionate, and restorative behavioral supports.

You likely already have a general understanding of the current ways in which staff are or are not yet implementing these five inclusive classroom practices in your system. You may have even spent significant resources to support staff regarding one, a few, or all of these practices. But to support your staff most effectively as you move your system toward greater inclusion, you will need to analyze your system data to identify staff strengths and growth areas related to the classroom practices shared here. (If you want additional learning and support regarding these powerful practices, please see the list of inclusive classroom practice resources in Appendix G, p. 123.)

Loop Back: In Chapter 2, you collected data that will help you to better understand where your system's strengths and growth areas are related to these specific inclusive classroom practices.

Use Your System Data to Identify Growth Areas

You will want to meet with your leadership team or inclusive steering committee to review data sets—on student achievement and discipline, from classroom observations, in the form of staff survey responses, and more. Some leaders find that tasking specific subcommittees from the inclusive steering committee or task force to analyze different data sets and report out findings is the most effective way to do this work. For example, one subcommittee might review the data on teacher and administrator perceptions of current inclusive practices and observational data of classroom walkthroughs while another subcommittee reviews student achievement data.

Once each subcommittee has analyzed data in detail and identified trends related to classroom practices, the larger committee will look across *all* data trends to highlight areas of strength and provide recommendations for growth. As soon as you have a better understanding of where your system needs support, it is time to create a systematic plan for robust professional development to empower your staff and build their capacity to provide effective classroom practices for all students.

Use the Data to Determine Professional Development

By an inclusive education expert

We have conducted equity reviews with school systems across the country—big and small, rural and urban—and have supported them in analyzing data, identifying key findings, and recommending resources related to creating inclusive schools. We often find that schools in a system vary widely in terms of implementing powerful inclusive practices, and that digging deeper into these differences helps leaders be strategic about planning PD.

We recommend breaking down key findings from your system analysis at the building, grade, and team levels to develop clarity about which staff need support on which inclusive practices. For example, in a medium-sized suburban district, we found that the elementary school staff were skilled at differentiation practices but needed guidance related to literacy instruction and behavioral supports. Meanwhile, the middle school staff needed training around behavioral supports, but had only recently begun to implement restorative behavioral practices with great success. This information not only helped the leadership team to design tailored PD across their system, but also helped staff feel seen and supported. The leadership was also able to build upon what was currently working and have staff from the elementary and middle schools observe one another, creating model classrooms and opportunities for collegial discussions. The leaders also created several cross-building professional learning communities (PLCs) to capitalize on staff expertise.

6.2: Develop a Systematic Plan for All-Staff Professional Development About Powerful Inclusive Classroom Practices

The success of your newly inclusive system will be bolstered by the quality of the PD opportunities you provide your staff to support collaboration, differentiation, adaptations, and natural and behavior supports. Your PD plan will need to be grounded in effective adult learning principles (Fink, 2013), individualized and relevant to staff (Sheridan et al., 2009), and delivered in a variety of ways with diverse pacing and levels of intensity (Cordingley et al., 2015). When you set out to create your PD plan, a single guiding question can support you and your leadership team: "How can our professional development and learning engage each teacher's mind and heart to improve classroom skills?" The answer to this question then guides leaders to set clear expectations for how to implement the plan and reconcile areas where new learning conflicts with current practice. Finally, it will be important to devise a strategy to examine the effectiveness of the PD offered to your staff and its impact on moving your system toward its inclusive vision.

Establish What You Need from PD

If the goal is to support your staff as they work seamlessly within an inclusive system, you will want to ensure that the PD plan is connected to your inclusive vision, including the "what" and "why" of inclusion as well as the "how" (e.g., the five powerful practices we discussed at the beginning of this chapter). As a leader, you will want to start with *what* your PD is teaching your staff about working toward inclusive educational opportunities for all students.

Over the years, we have seen very clear patterns emerge regarding the PD needs of systems as they undergo the inclusive change process. We have also found that it is helpful to break those patterns down into specific staff groupings of administrators, educators, related service providers, and paraprofessionals. Figure 6.1 outlines the most common PD needs for different staff groups.

Figure 6.1 Common PD Needs for Inclusive System Change by Staff Group

Staff Groups	Common PD Needs
Administrators	Staff need to learn . . . • What inclusion is. • Why inclusion is necessary. • How to create inclusive structures, services, schedules, and spaces. • How to lead and sustain change with strong emotional and ethical intelligence. • What drives adult behavior. • How to build trusting relationships. • How to engage authentically with others and create strong connections. • How to provide ongoing, just-in-time, and tiered or differentiated supports.
General and Special Education Teachers	Staff need to learn . . . • What inclusion is. • Why inclusion is necessary. • How to collaborate and co-teach. • How to differentiate. • How to provide adaptations. • How to provide natural supports. • How to provide behavioral supports. • Skills related to – Grading and assessment. – Utilization of supports. – Creating and implementing inclusive IEPs. – Training and supporting paraprofessionals. – Working with collaborative teams or related service providers. – Partnering with families.
Related Service Providers	Staff need to learn . . . • What inclusion is. • Why inclusion is necessary. • How to coach educators and co-teach with them. • How to develop inclusive IEP goals. • How to embed specially designed instruction into daily lessons and activities.
Paraprofessionals	Staff need to learn . . . • What inclusion is. • Why inclusion is necessary. • How to work as a member of a collaborative team. • How to provide accommodations and modifications. • How to support students with challenging behaviors. • How to provide natural and on-the-fly supports and how to fade adult support.

Essentials of Effective Inclusive PD

Once you have determined what you will address through PD by reviewing your own system data and the needs identified in Figure 6.1, you can begin to address *how* PD will be provided. The following six strategies for successful PD are grounded in the principles of effective adult learning (Fink, 2013).

Strategy 1: Commit to connection. As your staff adopt new inclusive practices, they need to feel connected and curious about what they are learning and expected to do. Ensure that PD content is directly connected to student success and the inclusive vision of the system and that it is concrete and addresses the daily challenges staff face. This way, staff can apply the new learning from PD immediately and see how it connects directly to their own growth toward more inclusive practices.

Strategy 2: Build in time to practice and apply new learning. Adult learners need sufficient support, practice, and real-life examples to learn and adopt new skills. Research shows that it takes adults 20 or more separate opportunities to practice a skill before they will be able to implement it (McManus, 2013). Space out the timing of PD so that staff can integrate what they have learned, try things out in the classroom, and discuss with colleagues.

Strategy 3: Provide differentiated PD. Your staff is just like a classroom full of students, learning in different ways, at different rates, and with different levels of interest in PD topics. One of the best ways to deliver PD is by differentiating and tailoring the support (Taylor, 2017). Using other tiered models as an example, you can start with the foundation topics that all staff will need and deliver it at the same time, with the same intensity. Ensure that most of the PD you offer is not siloed by staff group. Staff need multiple and varied opportunities to learn and grow together, even if they will move at different paces and learn in different ways.

A review of your system data (including staff discussions) should help you clarify which staff need more support and/or intensive PD and on which topics. For example, your elementary school teams may be ready to co-teach, but your middle school teams may still require concentrated study into co-teaching models that align with their schedule. Sometimes individual teams and/or subgroups will need more intensive PD than others, or PD that aligns with their exact content subject, experiences, or perspectives. For example, you may want to bring your physical education, music, and art teachers together with paraprofessionals to learn how to best utilize and leverage the latter's power when instructing large groups of students.

Strategy 4: Provide iterative feedback. All staff will need support at different stages of learning and with application of new skills. Start by setting expectations about what they need to implement from the PD offered. For example, all educational teams may be required to try one new co-teaching model after the training and be prepared to share their experiences at the next staff meeting. If the PD is more informational or inspirational, then the expectation may be for teams to attend the training and connect with colleagues.

Staff must know and expect that they will receive iterative feedback from you and other instructional mentors as they implement new practices to meet your set expectations. You will also want to give staff time to share and learn with their colleagues using PLCs (discussed further in the next section). Be sure to consistently connect all feedback to student success and the inclusive vision so that teachers are reminded of the goal of all their hard work.

Strategy 5: Get creative with time and methods. Staff PD can be delivered in all sorts of formats, group sizes, and lengths. You can provide PD in person or virtually; at the same time, "just in time," or on your own time. It can include podcasts, videos, conferences, book studies, social media, and online courses as well as coaching and problem-solving sessions, classroom walkabouts, or conversations with mentors and colleagues. Depending on your contractual agreements, PD can be paid or unpaid, or creative incentives can be offered (e.g., continuing education credits, classroom materials, office supplies, a free pass from bus duty). PD can take place in large groups, in small groups, in pairs, or individually; it can take place across five months, five hours, or even five minutes.

We recommend you record PD sessions (whether in person or virtual) and reuse them to maximize their impact. This will help you continue to create differentiated options for staff and allow greater flexibility with timing and access. For example, you may find that months after teaching staff about the "why" of inclusion, you are approaching new challenges and some staff are feeling resistant to the work. This might be a great time to revisit the "what" and "why" of inclusive education to reinspire and recommit your staff. Or you might be onboarding a new cohort of staff and want to revisit the basics of co-teaching and collaboration. Even highly inclusive districts need continued reminders of why the work is important.

Strategy 6: Provide ongoing PD for leaders. Professionals who are consistently at the "top of their game" tend to share common characteristics: They are coached regularly, seek continuous learning opportunities, and spend time honing their craft. Whether it's joining a leadership learning group, taking a course, reading a book, or making time to reflect, we find that the most effective leaders engage in their own ongoing PD. Any inclusive PD plan should also create systematic ways to grow the emotional and ethical intelligence of the systems' leaders and help them continue to effectively lead change, explore their implicit biases, and stay up to date on innovative classroom practices.

Utilize Powerful PD Opportunities

By a director of special education

Our district hosted a four-part series by Inclusive Schooling on the topic of differentiation. Sessions were held after school and recorded for later use. Some staff attended virtually; others watched the playback. Giving the staff two options for experiencing the sessions was helpful to their learning.

We further differentiated this learning experience by having one team take the activities from the sessions and build a presentation of their own. They then shared it with grade-level teams during PLC time. This option of using the information during PLC time helped create a format for discussion.

Additionally, we took one of the ideas from the PD sessions and created a "dinner menu" of professional development topics, including understanding and defining inclusion, co-teaching models, emotional regulation, and behavioral support. From the menu, staff could select not only the topic, but also their preferred learning format. Formats ranged from 1:1 coaching to exploring resources such as blogs, articles, and previously recorded PD content on their selected topic. Having so many options and choices for how to access this new information made our PD very powerful.

6.3: Create Learning That Gives Staff Opportunities to Learn with One Another and from Student Advocates and Inclusion Experts

After identifying the "what" of your PD offerings and committing to a deep understanding of the most effective ways to provide PD, you will need to create further learning opportunities that address both the hearts and the minds of your staff. Here, we show you ways to (1) create PLCs in which staff have time to collectively build their inclusive practices and skills, (2) explore how to more meaningfully use staff meeting time, (3) explicitly coach staff about changing practices, and (4) bring in voices of people who have walked the walk of inclusive system change.

Create PLCs to Grow Inclusive Practices

Growing and improving inclusive teaching practices does not occur one teacher at a time but collectively, and leaders can support this collective growth by creating purposeful PLCs (DuFour & Eaker, 2009). PLC work extends beyond the sacred collaborative planning time you have already provided your inclusive teams. During this work, leaders can direct teams to deeply connect student learning and instruction grounded in the inclusive classroom practices from the comprehensive inclusive PD plan. When establishing and guiding PLCs in a school, leaders should clearly share the purpose for the PLCs and outline expectations for and desired outcomes of PLC meetings. For example, PLC time might be used to unpack a recent PD session about designing differentiated lessons and creating adaptations for students with significant support needs. The PLC teams can answer questions such as "How can we create assessments that hold all students to high expectations while offering them flexible ways of demonstrating their knowledge?" or "If students with significant support needs experience barriers, how can we eliminate those barriers using adaptations and inclusive instructional design?" Essentially, the PLCs will work together to plan support strategies and instructional practices that ensure all students with significant disabilities can meaningfully access grade-level content and standards.

Staff Meetings: An Underutilized Opportunity for PD

We've all been at staff meetings that could have been emails, or were overtaken by someone's emotions, or were oriented toward problems rather than solutions. Yet as a leader, you know that it is necessary to bring your staff together to celebrate success, engage in shared meaning-making, communicate important information, and address legitimate concerns. We believe that your staff meetings are a golden opportunity for delivering just-in-time PD. Figure 6.2 (p. 90) describes four staff meeting PD strategies leaders can use to create additional opportunities for inclusive learning throughout the year.

Figure 6.2 Staff Meeting PD Strategies

Staff Meeting PD Strategy	Description
Model Demo	A staff member or team demonstrates a key practice either live or through video. For example, they might show a video of how they embed small groups across the daily routine versus only during a specified time and at small-group tables, or demonstrate a practice by roleplaying with colleagues or walking through their process.
Gallery Walk	This strategy requires a bit of pre-planning. Leaders create and share specific resources (e.g., lesson plans, video of co-teaching models in action, differentiation examples, creative behavioral support strategies) as exhibits around the room for staff to explore. It is helpful to include audio or video support or bulleted summaries of the resources. Once all staff have visited each item in the gallery, take a quick vote to decide which resources will be explored in greater depth at a future staff meeting or PLC or shared as a resource via email.
Problem Solving	This strategy has five steps, allows everyone to be heard, and keeps the group from spending the entire meeting admiring the problem without offering solutions. (1) Decide on a problem to solve. (2) Write the problem out clearly and in solvable form (e.g., "In what ways might we...?"). (3) Brainstorm solutions (try for 20 ideas or more). (4) Select a solution and create action steps. (5) Celebrate. Many school systems go through these five steps in 5- to 15-minute problem-solving rounds.
Learning Centers	Create learning centers that are highly relevant and engaging, include a wide variety of materials for learners at different stages, and are based upon interests. For example, if the focus is on differentiated grading, then there could be centers for differentiated rubrics, individual learning contracts, and report card writing for students with IEPs. Educators can rotate through each center for a broad range of ideas or select a specific center to begin their learning.

Coaching to Change Practice

Each staff member in a system will require different levels of support to truly put powerful inclusive practices to work in their classrooms. Some staff will learn about the practices and jump right in, but most will need additional support. To provide individual staff with the supports they will need to not only change but also sustain practice, leaders can step into the role of coach. Coaching aims to provide more intense support than all-staff PD or PLCs and can buoy staff at key moments when they are struggling or feel like they don't understand how to implement a specific practice. Coaching can be provided by administrators, existing instructional coaches, inclusion facilitators, or outside experts.

The first level of coaching utilizes differentiated opportunities to address different small-group needs. Some leaders create job-alike coaching groups. For example, they bring speech and language pathologists together and focus on supporting job-embedded needs like scheduling and inclusive service-delivery support. Other leaders might bring together groups of educators who are struggling with the same specific topic or practice (e.g., those who are struggling to create adaptations in mathematics). The coach then facilitates the session, helping the small job-alike or practice-alike groups to learn from each other, problem solve, and try out new strategies.

The more intense yet equally vital level of coaching is classroom-based coaching. Here, coaches observe lessons in person or review recorded lessons to address a specific topic. After the observation, the coaches and staff come together to discuss. For example, they might review and discuss the adaptations or differentiation of a lesson, or they might next do a lesson redesign or design the next lesson in sequence together. This level of support is particularly critical for teams that have a particular student with significant support needs; are collaborating with a co-teacher or related service provider in new ways and feeling stuck; need repeated practice making modifications or adaptations, supporting behavioral issues, or with differentiation in general; or need very specific examples using their specific context to understand how to implement new instructional strategies.

Learn from Those Who Have Walked the Walk

We have found that bringing in diverse voices, from students to inclusion experts, is a powerful way to reach the hearts and minds of staff as they learn more about inclusion and classroom practices. For example, one system created a panel of students with IEPs who talked about their experiences being supported by the district. When these self-advocates shared their experiences about being included or excluded in school, we tapped into the hearts of our staff and brought them back to the driving force behind all the work—the lives of their students. When we bring in inclusion experts to speak to the staff—those who have walked the walk of inclusive change and have worked day in and day out to implement, study, and teach about inclusive classroom practices—we are engaging the minds of staff in a deep and inspiring way with very helpful examples and tools of support.

6.4: Communicate Expectations to Staff and Provide Feedback on Those Expectations

Now that you have discussed how to set up your PD plan, we bring you back to the importance of providing clear expectations and iterative feedback for staff as they implement these new inclusive classroom practices. This often looks like scheduling observations of classroom practice and setting clear expectations about what you will be looking for in these observations. Use the Inclusive Classroom Observation Tool in Appendix C (p. 118) to support your collection of system data and conduct classroom observations or feedback sessions with staff connected directly to the five powerful inclusive classroom practices discussed earlier this chapter.

Feedback might also look like leaders sitting in on co-planning sessions with an inclusive team, joining in PLC meetings to provide support and face-to-face time, or meaningful use of the more intense coaching sessions to support individual teams or staff members. While this may all feel overwhelming for you, remember that leaders aren't the only system members who can provide ongoing and meaningful feedback. Use your *entire* staff strategically to provide feedback in a variety of ways—tap administrators, teacher leaders, existing coaches, and inclusion facilitators to provide observation and feedback support. And draw on the strengths of your system by implementing cross-classroom observations whereby staff can schedule and observe other educators or support staff and then give and receive feedback.

A final note on feedback: Focus on strengths and possibilities for your staff. Leaders are often trained to solve problems and can gravitate toward addressing needs or weakness rather than focusing on and building upon the strengths of their staff. But to give effective and successful feedback, leaders need to move beyond the idea of fixing or improving practice and, instead, bring a sense of possibility to their efforts. When giving feedback, always aim to create the opportunity for possibility by asking staff questions that focus on how to move them toward their dreams about classroom practices. Recognize and validate their core values. And give more of your attention to their strengths than to their weaknesses. When leaders see human possibilities, not human weaknesses, the results can be truly sustainable.

Evaluate Your PD Plan

Now that you've designed meaningful and ongoing opportunities for staff to receive feedback on new inclusive learning and new practices, you will need to devise a strategy to examine the effectiveness of your PD. Has the PD changed your system's classroom practices? Has it positively impacted student learning? To answer these questions, you will need to continue to collect and analyze your system data—classroom observational data, staff perception and feedback about PD and specific practices, and, of course, student achievement data. And don't forget that effective PD needs to focus on the hearts and minds of staff: When PD is working for staff, you can hear it, see it, and feel it. They will find it enjoyable and inspirational and look forward to more of it.

As the leader, it is both your responsibility and your privilege to compassionately support your staff's growth and development. The success of your new inclusive system depends on the quality of the ongoing PD opportunities you provide. This is where you'll want to most invest your time, money, and energy. Your PD plan should be focused on the five powerful inclusive practices, grounded in effective adult learning principles, individualized and relevant to staff, and delivered in a variety of ways. When you see your staff using innovative approaches to reaching and teaching all learners, you will feel how the inclusive path feels clearer, brighter, and more purposeful. You can truly see how the hearts, minds, and skills of your staff begin to shift and to align with the inclusive vision.

Be prepared to provide excellent PD for as long as it takes, and remember to loop back to great PD again and again—even the most inclusive systems continue to hone classroom practice to meet the unique needs of every student.

Milestone 6: Do our educators use powerful inclusive classroom practices?
Leadership Questions **Q 6.1** Does the leadership team understand the most powerful inclusive classroom practices? **Q 6.2** Does the leadership team have a highly effective professional development plan to address collaboration and co-teaching, differentiation, adaptations, and natural and behavioral supports? **Q 6.3** Does the leadership team provide staff with effective learning opportunities to support implementation of powerful inclusive classroom practices? **Q 6.4** Does the leadership team provide staff with feedback on powerful inclusive classroom practices to ensure accountability and meaningful support?

Milestone 6: Do our educators use powerful inclusive classroom practices?—(*continued*)
Leadership Steps **S 6.1** Explore highly effective inclusive classroom practices and identify growth opportunities. **S 6.2** Develop a systematic plan for all-staff professional development about powerful inclusive classroom practices. **S 6.3** Create learning that gives staff opportunities to learn with one another and from student advocates and inclusion experts. **S 6.4** Communicate expectations to staff and provide feedback on those expectations.

Consider your team's discussion around these questions and steps: Where is there clarity and where might your team need to focus additional time and energy? Then, turn to your Action Plan and add any necessary steps.

ACTION PLAN

Your Action Plan

Go to your Action Plan and record any necessary action steps.

7

Provide Ongoing Support

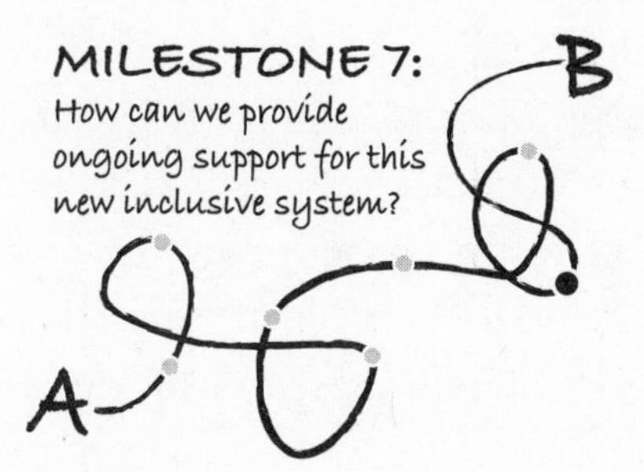

You have made it to the final milestone! We are celebrating you. We also want to acknowledge that even though we have outlined clear milestones in this book, inclusive school system reform is unlikely to follow a single linear path. You will likely loop forward and loop back multiple times as you address the seven milestones outlined in this book. This means that you are exactly where you need to be at this moment in time. It also means that you and all members of your school system will need ongoing support to continue to create a better system for all students.

In this final chapter, we explore the systems change process and inevitable human resistance to change. We provide insight into the human beings you are leading and offer our magical "Four *S*s of Leadership." We help you understand how to support staff through big emotions and how to systematically analyze educators' successes and needs, sustain your momentum, create habits for taking care of yourself, and, of course, celebrate it all along the way.

7.1: Explore Systems Change

Human beings tend to love predictability and fear change, which is rather unfortunate for those of us steeped in systems change work. When things are routine or unchanging, our bodily systems register a sense of safety and security. By contrast, change can disrupt our sense of homeostasis, threatening our sense of safety and security. We can then sometimes find ourselves in a "fight, flight, freeze, or faint" response. When you ask an entire school system made up of human beings to make changes—particularly to the teaching practices they use day to day, to the educational structures they work within, and to their very beliefs about education—a big disruption is bound to ensue.

Understand the Change Process

One of our favorite ways to depict how people move through change is the Change Cycle (Salerno & Brock, 2022; see the graphic at https://changecycle.com/change-cycle). The Change Cycle helps leaders understand that their team, staff, students, and families will experience a wide range of emotions, thoughts, and reactions to the changes required to create an inclusive system. Although not a one-size-fits-all depiction, the Change Cycle allows us to explore the range of feelings others are likely to experience. There are six stages to the Change Cycle:

1. **Loss:** Characterized by fear, caution, paralysis
2. **Doubt:** Characterized by resentment, skepticism, resistance
3. **Discomfort:** Characterized by anxiety, confusion, lack of productivity

DANGER ZONE

4. **Discovery:** Characterized by anticipation, resourcefulness, energy
5. **Understanding:** Characterized by confidence, pragmatism, productivity
6. **Integration:** Characterized by satisfaction, focus, generosity

Within each of the stages is a brief description of how people tend to feel, think, and behave at that stage. For example, in Stage 1, many people feel fear and have thoughts about going slower or decide not to change altogether. Sometimes these feelings and thoughts can lead to paralysis or a stalled period. In Stage 2, doubt creeps in and there can be feelings of resentment or skepticism toward the change. In inclusive system change, this can sound like "I really believe in inclusion, but not for *this* student." These thoughts and feelings often lead to resistance. Then, once humans make it through Stage 3, where there is anxiety, confusion, and a spinning of wheels, leaders are faced with the Danger Zone. This is a point in the change process where the pressure can feel too great, the risks too high, and the possibility of success unlikely. This is the point where leaders may decide to pump the brakes and stop the change. The Danger Zone is often where people go back to the way things were, regain their comfort even at the expense of others, and allow the status quo to remain.

But here's the good news: On the other side of the Danger Zone lies the opportunity to witness humans at their very best. The earlier feelings of anxiety shift to anticipation, confidence, and even satisfaction. Where there was once confusion, there is now creativity, a realistic response to challenges, and focused determination to make it all work. At this point in the change process, leaders begin to be surrounded by people who feel energized and productive and are generous with their time and talents. This is when real change takes place and everyone feels they are finally flourishing.

Ultimately, each system will go through its own unique ups and downs, creating its own cycle, spiral, or path to change. And when people don't fit a chosen model or framework like the one in Salerno and Brock's Change Cycle, leaders will need to continue searching for other ways to understand change in the context of their specific school community. No single graphic, model, or framework will apply to every situation, but knowing that there are cycles to the change process can help ensure you stay the course when things get difficult.

Understand Resistance

Resistance is a natural part of the change process. At one point or another, individuals or groups in your system will express skepticism, fear, anger, and doubt about the change process. You will likely hear resistance take the form of concerns like "We tried inclusion before and it didn't work," "They are going to dump everyone in my class without giving me any support," and the ever popular "This is going to negatively affect other students!" You will even experience pushback from your longest-serving and most-respected educators and families that have always had your back. We find that resistance can be one of the biggest obstacles for leaders to overcome because it can feel so personal, it can be loud, and it often threatens our progress. We can almost predict the number of times someone is going to pull you aside and say, "I'm not sure inclusion will work for my students" or "I think this particular group of students is better served over here or over there" or "Students with disabilities are not going to get what they need!"

Typically, these concerns come from a small group spread across your system. Within the first year of an inclusivity change process, we typically see what we call a 70-25-5 breakdown within communities focused on inclusive change: 70 percent of the community is on board (and past the Danger Zone), 25 percent is neutral about the changes, and 5 percent is unsure and still in Stages 1–3 of the Change Cycle, reacting with resistance to inclusive change. So, expect to hear these concerns from a small but loud corner of your system. Be prepared to listen, connect, and problem solve your way through rather than speaking back louder or with more information, as this approach can lead to increased pushback, resistance, and inertia (Berger, 2020). Effective leaders focus on the people behind the resistance, working to remove the barriers and stress that change can cause. Leaders can also begin to overcome resistance by building upon the momentum of the other 95 percent.

7.2: Learn More About How to Support Everyone Through Change

In this section, we describe a powerful way to support your school system through change and the inevitable resistance by focusing on individual human needs.

The Human Work Behind Change: The Four Ss of Leadership

If leaders don't understand the role of human needs and common adult human behavior during the change process, they can become frustrated and confused by the resistance of others. Across change theories, researchers, and frameworks, there is consensus that humans need to experience a sense of well-being, feel safe enough to be vulnerable, and accept different ways of doing things to change and eventually thrive in a new system.

From Abraham Maslow to Rick Hanson to Brené Brown, researchers have surfaced a wide variety of human needs across different frameworks. All of us have needs for autonomy, belonging, certainty, comfort, connection, contribution, emotional safety, growth, independence, love, mastery, respect, satisfaction, and significance. The human need for certainty, which often feels distant or even impossible during systemwide change, can create stress that, when unchecked, can lead to reactive behaviors that range from anger and frustration to confusion, depression, and exhaustion. When needs aren't met, and when we struggle to manage the energy and tension (that is, the stress) in our bodies, we often react by going into a "fight, flight, freeze, or faint" response.

As a leader, you want to make sure to meet individuals in your system who struggle with the stressors of change with kindness and support and look for ways to satisfy their needs. To guide you in this work, we've fine-tuned a framework that includes specific strategies for addressing the needs of the wide variety of humans you will lead through the change process. Our Four *S*s of Leadership framework (Causton & Pretti-Frontczak, 2021c) is grounded in neuroscience and particularly in Dan Siegel and Tina Payne Bryson's work on attachment science (Siegel & Bryson, 2020).

Figure 7.1 outlines the Four *S*s of Leadership and identifies specific strategies you can use to help your staff, families, community, and even board members and students meet their needs during the inclusive change process.

Figure 7.1 The Four Ss of Leadership

The Four Ss	Related Leadership Strategies
Safe: I protect those I serve, shield them from emotional harm, and avoid being a source of threat or fear.	• Notice what others need and are trying to communicate. • Validate people's emotions. • Offer individualized choices. • Give people time to process ideas and emotions. • Invite calm by being calm.
Seen: I notice and see others through their wholeness.	• Listen to understand and avoid judgment. • Slow down and avoid rushing to fix things. • Allow for the processing of emotions and offer and/or invite people to employ coping strategies. • Be aware of your own biases, power, and privilege in the situation. • Notice and see the human behind the behavior.
Soothed: I help others to be calm and responsive.	• Acknowledge how others feel and allow them time and space to process emotions. • Recognize and reduce stressors. • Monitor your tone of voice and facial expressions. • Use empathetic, nonverbal communication (e.g., slower speech, an inviting posture, welcoming gestures, soft eyes). • Ask questions that demonstrate your desire to understand others' perspectives (e.g., "Can you tell me more about...?").
Secure: I help others experience a sense of well-being and of support as they overcome challenges and take action.	• Get curious about your own reactions and be aware of your own biases. • Connect emotionally with others by being authentic and open-hearted. • Be reliable and consistent; set clear boundaries that still breathe. • Help people find creative solutions to problems. • Allow for a fresh start—forgive when needed. • Acknowledge and repair harm when necessary.

Source: From *The Four Ss of Leadership* by J. Causton & K. Pretti-Frontczak, 2021, Inclusive Schooling. Copyright 2021 by Inclusive Schooling. Reprinted with permission.

Support Your Staff Through Big Emotions

As we've already discussed, change of any kind can cause big emotions. This might look like someone yelling at you during a meeting, bringing the union into the conversation, crying, shaming or publicly blaming you, or even withdrawing from playing an active role in the change process. You might even hear from the union or association leaders who think that the change has come too fast or that you should recalibrate or rethink things before going any further.

You will recognize the big emotions right away. They are often the most uncomfortable part of inclusive change work. To help you navigate them, here are a few more strategies. Start by not only expecting but also allowing the people you work with to feel the big emotions. Hold space and show compassion rather than feeling defensive, rushing to fix the issue, aiming to alleviate their suffering, or even giving advice (yet). Next, your aim is to connect with people by validating their emotions and expressing empathy. Again, avoid getting defensive or annoyed, and ensure they feel seen. Once you have allowed for the big emotion and made attempts to connect to and soothe those experiencing it, your aim is to co-regulate and invite them back into a more responsive state. You do this by remaining calm and soothing their system. When people are in a more regulated state and have been able to process their emotions, they are more likely to be ready to engage in problem solving, or at least talking through what they might need going forward. Once people feel safe, seen, and soothed, your secure relationship with them allows for brainstorming, dreaming, beta testing, advice giving, and problem solving. Supporting staff thoughtfully through big emotions is one of the most effective ways to help them understand that you can support them through the difficulties of inclusive change.

Lead with Integrity

By a school superintendent

As school leaders, our integrity is constantly on display. It is evident through communication with staff, during interactions with parents, through participation in board meetings, and in how we communicate ideas and information. It is also on display during classroom visits, in meetings, and in how we listen to others. People are always watching, and they are looking for clues about who their leader is and what the leader believes in. We want to support you strongly, clearly, and compassionately so you can uphold your vision for inclusive change with integrity.

Consider the high level of trust being sought from staff, parents, and students to transform their entire concept of education. As a leader, you are challenging the ideas of which students are worthy and capable of learning in the general education setting and which students are not capable and will be relegated to separate spaces. This type of change in thinking is foundation-shaking!

Leading with integrity means doing what you say you will. It's walking the talk. If you tell your staff that they will receive professional development, make sure it happens! If you believe that common planning time is important, give it to them! If you adopt the belief that all means all, then students should not be placed elsewhere. If people have questions, stay as long as it takes, tap the right supporters and mentors, and get folks the answers.

7.3: Design a Systematic Way to Analyze Educators' Successes and Needs

To help your staff be seen and heard, especially when challenges arise or motivation wanes, you will need to create a systematic way to learn what is working for staff and where they need more or different support. Here, we share five ways to analyze educators' successes and needs.

Strategy 1: Keep gathering data. Gather a variety of data to inform your decisions in a variety of ways. Show up often and hold listening sessions. When possible, schedule lunch-and-learn sessions or hold after-school office hours. Collect staff perception data using short surveys. Collect observational walkthrough data to understand how staff are using inclusive practices in the classroom. Build in ways to continuously check in with students, families, board members, and so on as you continue to review your most current service-delivery maps and student achievement and behavior data.

Strategy 2: Keep seeing the whole system as well as each of the parts. You will be able to do the most with the data you've collected if you narrow your analysis. Begin at the system level, then the school level, then grade-level teams, and finally co-teaching groups. When your system is composed of many teams, grades, and buildings, you will see that groups often travel at different paces and in different ways through the change process. That is to be expected and embraced.

Same Goal, Different Pace

By a director of special education

Our district had our early childhood, elementary school, and middle school teams, all of which were at different levels of readiness to engage in this work. Even within our elementary schools, there were differences between buildings that housed our self-contained classrooms and those that did not. Our vision is to have all schools implementing equitable access to inclusive education for all our students.

To achieve this vision in our district, we let each school set a path toward inclusion that recognized its own baseline. We didn't limit or reduce our sense of urgency or allow for choice about going on the journey. Rather, we allowed for choice about the path. The work of the inclusion steering committee was building-specific, using the Inclusive System Change Path and developing action plans and goals that were individualized to meet building-level needs. Some of our buildings focused heavily on mindset change, while others felt they were ready to move swiftly and started making structural changes and instructional practice changes.

Giving buildings autonomy to move where they needed based on their staff and students really helped with ownership over the change process. It allowed some buildings to take appropriate and manageable steps while giving other buildings more freedom to move at a quicker pace. And all along, each building knew that we were all becoming inclusive.

Strategy 3: Keep planning how best to provide support. Offer a variety of support options that will both meet staff needs and give staff agency over their own learning and successes. One idea to allow for just-right support is to provide a PD menu of options for staff to choose from or schedule a range of lunch-and-learn topics staff can attend. You might even offer staff the time to host an "unconference," where they can use the system data to collaborate with one another to meet identified needs and share ideas across teams and buildings.

Strategy 4: Keep keeping it open. We recommend having an open-door policy in place and being available to staff when they need support. This helps staff to feel comfortable stopping by and potentially interrupting you to discuss or brainstorm ideas and solutions. One special education administrator we worked with had office hours in every single building; staff would sign up for slots and come in to sit and talk about what was on their hearts and minds. They knew that the leader would be in their building every week, and the time slots could be for individuals or teams. Staff members who aren't coming through your door, emailing you, calling you, or signing up to problem solve will still require connection and support. Make sure you have a variety of ways for people to connect with you to tell you about barriers and celebrate successes.

Strategy 5: Keep giving meaningful feedback. In addition to taking advantage of all the feedback opportunities and tools we shared in Chapter 6, you will want to create a plan to provide feedback for staff about the successes and needs of the system. To do this, you might host problem-solving sessions, create a living Q&A document that everyone contributes to, or conduct stop-by co-planning meetings and PLC sessions. No matter the feedback mechanism, be sure to build upon the strengths of the system and your staff by using an "assets and opportunities approach" by focusing on what is going well and moving toward the next growth opportunity. Ask questions such as "What's working right now?" "Can you tell me about a time when you felt the best about your work?" or "What is your wish for the rest of the year?"

Loop Back: Return to Chapter 6 for a deeper dive into providing meaningful feedback for staff, or loop forward to the end of this chapter to consider options for celebratory feedback.

Quarterly Data Review

By a school superintendent

Our learning and teaching team creates ongoing opportunities for all school and district leaders to engage with student data. The goal of this time together is to learn, grow, and celebrate. We start each data-review meeting by reviewing our collective commitment to inclusion and student success. We commit to practicing, rehearsing the work, monitoring results, and expecting continuous improvement.

When a school or district makes a collective commitment to each student, it is incumbent upon the leaders to make system data visible. We do this with great intentionality and create a safe place for our leaders to be vulnerable and recognize that we are all in a different place on the inclusivity journey.

We then engage in a virtual gallery walk using our system data—longitudinal district data by domain, districtwide grade-level data, fall-to-winter data. We also look at each school's comprehensive data and grade-level data, observational walkthrough data, teacher feedback, and service-delivery maps. Before leaders begin the gallery walk, we ask them to reflect on several questions:

- In what areas did our students do well?
- How are system structures and practices prompting our inclusive vision?
- What are our areas of need?
- What questions do you have about another school's growth?

I believe that our commitment to monitoring our progress, learning from one another, and celebrating has often laid the foundation for our success. Yes, we have long-term system goals, but getting to see and celebrate short-term goals and successes is what really fuels the engine of change. Like our students, adults need to see growth and progress toward their goals.

The following are sample findings from our most recent data review meeting.

Areas where our district did well:

- Double-digit growth in grades K–5 in reading in all but one grade level
- An increase in kindergarten reading proficiency of 35 percentage points
- Participation by high school students with complex support needs in grade-level content classes

Ways our system structures are aligning to our inclusive vision:

- The autism program no longer exists at the elementary school.
- The middle school 7th and 8th grade teams are all co-teaching.
- We have only one self-contained room at the high school, and students are getting out to general education classes throughout the day.
- We have a clear plan to schedule all students out of that self-contained room next semester.

Areas of need:

- Reading instruction in grades 6–8 represents an opportunity for staff growth, as students only experienced single-digit growth.
- Staff can focus on K–8 vocabulary, which will help increase comprehension.
- High school LRE data is not as inclusive as that of the middle school or the three elementary schools.

Questions about schools' growth:

- What is the elementary school doing in 5th grade to grow its readers? 24 percent growth, wow!

- What is K. doing to get 50 percent growth with her students for reading?
- What instructional strategies for math and reading are middle school 8th grade teams implementing?
- What instructional support strategies did the MS leaders provide general education teachers as they welcomed more students with significant disabilities into their classes?

7.4: Determine Ways to Sustain the Momentum of Change

At some point in your journey, you will begin to see change happening in your system, but new challenges will also arise. Some will celebrate and some will push back all over again. Certain administrators will excitedly talk about their reading scores and LRE data while others will ask questions such as "Should we turn back?" This is the crucial time when your visible, present, and unwavering support of inclusive work will keep the change process moving forward. Stay the course and hold true to your vision. It may feel easier to let go and give in to the resistance or the challenges. We know! But research shows there are virtually no documented instances of schools improving outcomes for students without intervention by talented leaders (DeVita et al., 2007). So, although you may feel like you are trudging uphill in the snow with no shoes, remember that (1) *you* and your talents are critical to success and (2) others have gone before you and can show you the way.

The following are field-tested ways to sustain your momentum through your entire change journey.

Strategy 1: Show up and listen. Visit each school and find times to be with your school leaders. Sit with your department chairs to listen and see the successes, challenges, and barriers that are present. When you walk into your schools and classrooms, remember that this is not about you, but about listening to your staff. Listen to the 1st grade teacher who is frustrated because he has never encountered the types of challenging behaviors that he's dealing with now. Listen to his fear, learn what is happening. Validate staff and let them know you will use the information to provide support. Showing up isn't only a "sometimes" thing. This is a practice that you will want to schedule on a regular basis. Be present. Be vulnerable. Be a learner. Repeat.

Strategy 2: Embrace difficult conversations. Be ready to listen openly to concerns and remind folks that they are capable and you believe in them.

Recognize their frustrations and respond by providing feedback and support. Reiterate that inclusion of students with disabilities is not negotiable but that you will be there to guide them.

Strategy 3: Take in concerns to fix the system. The need for systems change is often revealed in the form of individual concerns—for example, a teacher's belief that students with certain needs don't belong in general education. When concerns about inclusive changes arise, it is helpful to reframe them not as problems related to a specific student or staff issue but as system issues that can be supported through additional resources, time, professional development, planning, and so on.

System Comebacks

By a director of special education

1. We often hear that inclusion is great for most students, but "it's just not for this one kid." In response, we always refer to our definition of inclusive education and share that the focus is never on student deficits and always on the systems, supports, and structures of a building or classroom. So, instead of saying inclusion isn't right for this student, we instead say that our building systems, supports, and structures are creating a barrier to include all students. The focus is and should be on how we fix our systems, supports, and structures, rather than the student.

2. When having conversations about removing students from the general education classroom, some staff focus on the deficits of students or seem to believe that there is a qualifying criterion for inclusion, such as being able to stay seated or knowing all letter sounds. In these cases, discussing what we have done to allow for choice in seating arrangements or how we have supported the student through academic differentiation holds teams to the IDEA requirement of exhausting all supports before removal. By using more collaboration and learning from others, we can problem solve about appropriate supports earlier to avoid exhausting *ourselves*.

3. Some educators continued to see inclusion as a "special education thing" or something "just" for special education students. As leaders, we must talk about inclusive change as a systemwide transformation that begins with helping *all* educators and school personnel reach *all* students. This means special and general educators, related service providers, paraprofessionals, and school

personnel like bus drivers, administrative assistants, and volunteers all need clarity about the importance of their role in moving toward inclusion.

Take Care of *You*

As a leader, you are constantly considering the needs of your staff, students, and families. But who will support *you* when undergoing the challenging work of inclusive change? We know from experience that changing a system in pursuit of equity is likely to be one of the most challenging tasks of your career. Consider the following questions when thinking about your own self-care during this journey:

- **"What professional allies and supporters can I rely on when I have questions or am feeling frustrated?"** We encourage you to schedule times to interact with these individuals. This doesn't need to happen through formal meetings, and in fact, it's probably better if it doesn't. Plan to grab coffee, chat on the phone, or visit them after school. The schedules of busy administrators fill quickly, so mark this on your calendar and prioritize it just as you would anything else. It may just be your most important meeting of the week.
- **"Who has walked this path before me?"** Finding colleagues to talk to who have similar visions and ideals can help on the lonely path to change. They can provide encouragement and emotional support and can help problem solve or even help you to recommit to your values. Communicating with colleagues who have already completed or are currently engaged in this work will help to dissolve any sense of loneliness.
- **"To whom can I delegate certain tasks and with whom can I share responsibilities?"** Think about the members of your guiding coalition who can share the burden of work with you. Not only is this an important part of self-care, but it is also critical to building capacity and shared understanding.
- **"How can I nourish myself with positive feedback?"** You *will* hear from staff who are starting to see the benefits of inclusive change. You'll hear about elementary school students engaging in learning activities when no one thought they ever would, or about high school students eating lunch with their peers rather than in the life skills room and

developing friendships in general education classes. Let these conversations nourish you. Write them down. Revisit them as often as you want.

- **"What activities or supports do I have outside school?"** Reflect on your personal support network and the things that give you joy. Come up with a plan for protecting these times so that work doesn't become all-consuming. For example, turn off the email on your phone for a few hours when you get home from work—if there is a true emergency, someone will call you. Set aside work-free blocks of time on the weekends to focus on family, yourself, and/or your community. Set boundaries to protect your mental health. When we set aside time for ourselves, our families, and our friendships, we are consciously cultivating an essential connection to important aspects of our nonwork lives.

We know it may be hard to prioritize yourself as a system leader—especially when you are in the middle of an inclusive change process. But self-care truly is critical. When we commit to sustaining healthy emotional, cognitive, and spiritual parts of ourselves, it is easier for us to share our time, knowledge, and compassion with others at work. This not only helps to keep the pressures and huge responsibilities of leadership work at bay, but also increases our presence of mind and energy levels. We have more to give to others, our patience levels are higher, and we can function better for ourselves, our loved ones, and those in our care within our school system.

7.5: Create Genuine Systems of Celebration

So, you are taking care of yourself and your staff is on the path to an inclusive system. Make sure you pause often to celebrate wildly and proudly! Celebrate the little moments, the big moments, the milestones, the quarter-milestones, and even the setbacks that led to deeper understanding. We recommend creating an infrastructure for formal celebrations as well as making space for informal, in-the-moment celebrations. You want to be sure that every member of the system community sees the successful changes happening for students, staff, families, and the larger community. Celebration is the ritual that will keep your momentum going and help everyone stay positive and productive. Use any of the following ideas to inspire you and grow your own "system of celebration."

- **Recommitment Meetings:** One school system we know holds a recommitment meeting each year to celebrate all their inclusive accomplishments and decide if the vision statement needs revising. They use the meeting as a time to re-energize their work of holding one another accountable, removing obstacles, and courageously and consistently disrupting beliefs and practices that do not support their inclusive vision.

- **Digital Storytelling:** Many systems we know share and celebrate their successes using digital storytelling through photos, videos, slideshows, and so on. One large school system we know even created an inclusion film that they played at the kickoff of the school year. It showcased inclusion in action throughout the system. There was dancing, singing, students talking about their experiences—it was amazing!
- **Snack and Share:** A system leader we know found out that many of the system's educators were voluntarily meeting before and after school. To encourage collaboration across schools, she decided to host snack-and-share events where staff teams could come together to meet and share their ideas, celebrate, and leverage shared resources while enjoying free snacks from the district. You can also turn this idea into free snacks during in-school planning meetings or even after school.
- **Inclusion Hype Person:** Assign someone to be your inclusion "hype person." This is basically a person who shares the news of inclusion. (It could be a hype team, too.) Let people know all about the good work going on and highlight successes.
- **Inclusion Oscars:** One system we worked with had an inclusion-related Academy Awards–style event at the end of the year. Staff used simple school supplies to create awards for one another and held the ceremony in the library with a red carpet and paparazzi.
- **Inclusion Party:** Celebrate all improvements in your system's data that measures inclusion. Host LRE parties when you bring a student back from being placed out of district. Celebrate the closing of a self-contained room or program. Make toasts to new inclusive teams.
- **"You've Got Skills, They're Multiplying":** Notice and celebrate new skills and staff efforts to try new things. This type of celebration can be on the fly, during staff meetings, or at a formal school event. The point is to show off how teams are trying new things like co-teaching, differentiated assessments, and compassionate behavior supports. Sometimes the attempts will be messy, sometimes they will flop, but be sure to celebrate the effort and the risk!
- **Shout It from the Rooftops:** Share successes from student, family, and staff voices. For example, every time you get a positive email from

a parent or a big accomplishment from a student, share it in any format that will be powerful (e.g., in your newsletter, emails, blogs, meetings, messages to the board of education, updates, and daily communications). You might need to purchase a bullhorn.

- **Thank-A-Thon:** This is an event (or a staff meeting) where everyone writes or texts or calls people in the system to thank them for something specific that they have been doing to create inclusive spaces and practices. Systematically write meaningful notes of gratitude to individuals and teams and deliver them in person.
- **Rainbow Milestone Party:** One team has a color-themed milestone party: red for Milestone 1, orange for Milestone 2, and so on. They dress in these colors and make color-themed food. (OK, as far as we know, no one has done this yet, but you could be the first!)

Flash mobs, dress up-days, hot chocolate toasts, popcorn days, cheese days, hat days—you name it, you can turn it into a celebration. These can be standalone events, or better yet, you can turn them into a routine part of the life and soul of your system. For example, every Monday staff meeting (or even better, every Tuesday staff meeting) starts or ends with a celebration (or is bookended by them). Every month you host a Thank-A-Thon. The potential for routine celebration is endless!

You can support your system, your staff, and yourself in small and big ways, from helping individual staff deal with big emotions to building sacred time for meaningful data review, feedback, and celebrations. In this final chapter, we explored the systems change process, the reasons human beings push back against change, our Four *S*s of Leadership, and strategies from other leaders on how to systematically analyze educators' successes and needs, sustain your momentum, and celebrate throughout your inclusive journey.

And right now, we are celebrating *you,* dear reader, for getting to the end of this book, for being as excited about inclusion as we are. We are celebrating you for creating your Action Plan at every milestone. Even if you are saying to yourself, "What Action Plan?" we celebrate you for finding it in Appendix A and starting it.

Congratulations on your growth, your journey, and all the success that will come to you, your staff, your school community, and, most important, your students. Here is to you.

Now, onward!

Milestone 7: How can we provide ongoing support for this new inclusive system?
Leadership Questions **Q 7.1** Does the leadership team understand systems change? **Q 7.2** Does the leadership team understand how to support everyone through change? **Q 7.3** Does the leadership team have a systematic way to analyze educators' successes and needs? **Q 7.4** Does the leadership team have a way to sustain the momentum of change? **Q 7.5** Does the leadership team document progress and celebrate often?
Leadership Steps **S 7.1** Explore systems change. **S 7.2** Learn more about how to support everyone through change. **S 7.3** Design a systematic way to analyze educators' successes and needs. **S 7.4** Determine ways to sustain the momentum of change. **S 7.5** Create genuine systems of celebration.

Consider your team's discussion around these questions and steps: Where is there clarity and where might your team need to focus additional time and energy? Then, turn to your Action Plan and add any necessary steps.

Your Action Plan

Go to your Action Plan and record any necessary action steps.

Appendixes

The resources included in these Appendixes are available for download at www.inclusiveschooling.com/the-way-to-inclusion and at www.ascd.org/the-way-to-inclusion-resources.

Appendix A: Your Action Plan

Action Step	Measurement	Deadline	Person Responsible
Milestone 1: Do we understand why inclusive education is the way forward?			
Milestone 2: Have we seen our system through an equity lens?			
Milestone 3: Do we have a clear public vision for inclusion and understanding of the needed system-level changes?			
Milestone 4: How can we realign existing service-delivery structures to create an inclusive system?			
Milestone 5: How can we reimagine schedules and collaborative staff roles?			
Milestone 6: Do our educators use powerful inclusive classroom practices?			
Milestone 7: How can we provide ongoing support for this new inclusive system?			

Appendix B: Equity Review Data Collection Guide

General System Demographic Data

1. Number of total students in the system	
2. Number and percentage of students with IEPs in the system	
3. LRE data for the system	80% or more in general education: 40–79% in general education: Less than 40% in general education: In district school outside of home building: Out of district:
4. Number of special education teachers at each school and their special education positions/titles (e.g., resource teacher, self-contained teacher, co-teacher, resource/co-teacher)	
5. Number of general education teachers at each school	
6. Number of related service providers (e.g., OT, PT, SLP, psychologist) and specialists (e.g., literacy, math, multilingual language, gifted and talented) at each school	

7. Number of special education paraprofessionals at each school and specific positions/titles (you can also include the number of non-special education paraprofessionals)	

Student Socioeconomic Data

8. Number and percentage of students who qualify for free or reduced-price lunch in the system	
9. Number and percentage of students with IEPs who qualify for free or reduced-price lunch	
10. Number and percentage of students with IEPs in specific LRE categories who qualify for free or reduced-price lunch	80% or more in general education: 40–79% in general education: Less than 40% in general education: In district school outside of home building: Out of district:

Student Race or Ethnicity Data

Note: Though race and ethnicity are separate constructs, both are reflected in the categories used by the U.S. Office of Special Education to request and track specific student demographic data.

11. Number and percentage of students of color in your system (broken down by race or ethnicity)	
12. Number and percentage of students of color in your system with IEPs (broken down by race or ethnicity)	

13. Number and percentage of students of color with IEPs in specific LRE categories	80% or more in general education: 40–79% in general education: Less than 40% in general education: In district school outside of home building: Out of district:

Disability Label Data

14. Number of students with specific disability labels in your system; you can further break this data down by demographic category (e.g., students with IEPs, race/ethnicity, eligibility for free or reduced-price lunch, multilingual learners)	
15. Number of students with specific disability labels in specific LRE categories; you can further break this data down by demographic category (e.g., students with IEPs, race/ethnicity, eligibility for free or reduced-price lunch, multilingual learners)	80% or more in general education: 40–79% in general education: Less than 40% in general education: In district school outside of home building: Out of district:

Achievement Data

16. Graduation rate broken down by demographic category (e.g., students with IEPs, race/ethnicity, eligibility for free or reduced-price lunch, multilingual learners)	
17. Standardized assessment data broken down by demographic category (e.g., students with IEPs, race/ethnicity, eligibility for free or reduced-price lunch, multilingual learners)	

18. Dropout rate broken down by demographic category (e.g., students with IEPs, race/ethnicity, eligibility for free or reduced-price lunch, multilingual learners)	

Behavioral Data

19. Number of disciplinary actions (by type) for all students in the system	
20. Number of disciplinary actions (by type) broken down by demographic category (e.g., students with IEPs, race/ethnicity, eligibility for free or reduced-price lunch, multilingual learners)	

Qualitative Data

Classroom Visits	The leadership team can conduct classroom visits of all educational settings to better understand how staff is used in each classroom and what instructional practices occur. We recommend using the Inclusive Classroom Observation Tool in Appendix C (p. 118) to maintain consistent observational data.
A Day in the Life of a Student	Each member of the leadership team can select a student and compile qualitative data about what that student experiences in a single school day—anything from social and hallway experiences to classroom instructional practices, types of adult support, or even time spent in or out of general education. It is helpful for the team to select diverse students in terms of disability, race/ethnicity, language, gender expression, and age. One district we worked with had staff (and students) identify students who were thriving in the system. They studied factors that contributed to their success to increase opportunities for all.
Surveys and/or Focus Groups	The leadership team can share a survey with the system community members and/or hold focus groups with staff, families, and students. This data collection helps the leadership team to understand how these diverse groups understand inclusion practices, structures, and supports. We recommend using the Inclusive System Focus Group Survey in Appendix D (p. 120) to guide you or create your own.

Source: From *Equity Review Data Collection Guide* by J. Causton and K. MacLeod, 2022, Inclusive Schooling.

Appendix C: Inclusive Classroom Observation Tool

Teacher(s): ____________________

Grade(s): ________

Type of Support Services: Gen. Ed. __________ Co-teaching __________

Adults: Gen. Ed. __________ Special Ed. __________ Inclusion Facilitator __________

Specialist __________ Para. (#) __________ Related Service __________ Other __________

Lesson Topic:

Evidence of Standards-Based Instruction:

Evidence of Individualized Goals for Students with Complex Support Needs:

Staff use varied collaborative teaching models such as station, one-teach/one-make multisensory, parallel, duet, and one-teach/ one-assist or float.	☐ Not evident ☐ Emerging ☐ Evident ☐ Highly evident	**Observation Notes**
Staff use varied instructional formats such as whole class, small group, pairs.	☐ Not evident ☐ Emerging ☐ Evident ☐ Highly evident	**Observation Notes**
Staff work with all students.	☐ Not evident ☐ Emerging ☐ Evident ☐ Highly evident	**Observation Notes**
Student grouping is heterogeneous; groups change often; homogeneous groups are used sparingly, if at all.	☐ Not evident ☐ Emerging ☐ Evident ☐ Highly evident	**Observation Notes**
Staff provide appropriate adaptations for students with disabilities.	☐ Not evident ☐ Emerging ☐ Evident ☐ Highly evident	**Observation Notes**

Instruction is differentiated and students have multiple ways to access content, process learning, and show what they know. Check examples of access points provided: ☐ Visuals ☐ Audio ☐ Video ☐ Modeling ☐ Objects/manipulatives ☐ Technology ☐ Varied levels of technology ☐ Opportunities for practice ☐ Multiple learning strategies ☐ Culturally relevant content ☐ Student choice ☐ AAC ☐ Other: ______________	☐ Not evident ☐ Emerging ☐ Evident ☐ Highly evident	**Observation Notes**
Staff facilitate peer relationships and support.	☐ Not evident ☐ Emerging ☐ Evident ☐ Highly evident	**Observation Notes**
Staff provide all students with environmental supports such as flexible seating, designated space for movement, and easy access to adaptations and communication supports.	☐ Not evident ☐ Emerging ☐ Evident ☐ Highly evident	**Observation Notes**
Staff provide thoughtful, compassionate, and positive supports for students with challenging behaviors.	☐ Not evident ☐ Emerging ☐ Evident ☐ Highly evident	**Observation Notes**

Source: From *Inclusive Classroom Observation Tool* by J. Causton and K. MacLeod, 2022, Inclusive Schooling. Copyright 2022 by Inclusive Schooling. Reprinted with permission.

Appendix D: Inclusive System Focus Group Survey

1. What is your perception of the district's mission around inclusive education?

2. What evidence do you already have that inclusive education is in place?

3. How do you feel about the district's shift toward more inclusive service delivery and practices? What does the shift mean to you?

4. Can you describe ways in which students are full members of the school community?

5. Can you describe ways in which school leaders discuss and support expectations for staff collaboration and student inclusion?

6. (For staff that are already co-teaching or part of inclusive teams:) Do you feel like you are able to co-plan instruction and support for students with colleagues regularly? Do you feel you have sufficient support (time, professional development, feedback) available to support quality planning and co-teaching?

7. How are you thinking or feeling about general and special education teachers having a shared ownership for all students?

8. Do you feel knowledgeable about the contents of the IEPs for students you support? What supports have you received or would you like to receive about IEPs?

9. How do you create and use adaptations such as accommodations and modifications and other classroom supports to educate all students in the general education classroom?

10. Are related services personnel supporting students within the general education classroom and consulting with educators? Will you be able to describe your experience or perception of this service-delivery model in the future?

11. Are you aware of any schoolwide behavioral support systems in place either for all students or specifically for students with disabilities?

12. Can you describe the supports you have or would need from leaders to effectively collaborate with colleagues and include all students?

13. How does the school or district celebrate diversity?

14. How do staff members work to create an atmosphere where human difference is understood and appreciated?

15. Do you think all teachers have an understanding of disability and support needs?

16. Do you think families feel welcomed and valued in the educational process and the move toward more inclusion?

17. Do you have concerns, or do you anticipate a more inclusive service-delivery model?

18. What questions about inclusive service delivery do you have?

Source: From *Inclusive System Focus Group Survey* by J. Causton and K. MacLeod, 2022, Inclusive Schooling.

Appendix E: Inclusive System Scheduling Process

Phase 1: Schedule Students into General Education Classrooms	
Step ①:	Start by scheduling students with significant support needs into classrooms. Make sure they are spread across general education classrooms and not clustered, using natural proportions as your guide.
Step ②:	Next, consider all students' support needs. **Step 2a: Consider levels of support.** Inclusion facilitators might support students with more significant needs, co-teachers might support students with medium to high support needs, and consultative services might support students with low to medium needs. **Step 2b: Consider cross-categorical support.** In a cross-categorical approach, special education teachers support all students with IEPs regardless of disability label or level of need. Leaders can divide up teacher caseloads equally or in a way that makes sense for educator workload using flexible roles to meet the needs of students.
Step ③:	Create balanced and diverse general education classes by placing students with a range of academic, behavioral, and social-emotional needs across classes.
Step ④:	Strategically assign students to general education classrooms so they have access to the necessary staff and levels of support (e.g., co-teachers, consultative services, inclusion facilitators).
Step ⑤:	Assign groups of students to specific general education classes based on related service needs.
Step ⑥:	Strategically place students in general education classes who do not have disability labels but have other significant needs, being careful not to create classes that have high percentages of students with significant needs.
Step ⑦:	Assign all other students without disability labels heterogeneously to general education classrooms.
Phase 2: Schedule Educators and Related Service Providers	
Step ①:	Review how many members of your potential staff there are: special educators, related service providers, gifted and talented educators, educators of multilingual learners, Title 1 educators, reading specialists, coaches, and so on.
Step ②:	Assign staff based on inclusive support structures and student needs (e.g., co-teachers, consultative services, inclusion facilitators), not labels.
Step ③:	Assign staff to classes and to students considering both caseloads and workloads.
Step ④:	Reduce the number of different classrooms that a single educator or related service provider supports.
Step ⑤:	Reduce the number of buildings and classrooms that educators and related service providers support.
Step ⑥:	Create common and meaningful planning time by aligning preparation or planning periods.
Phase 3: Schedule Paraprofessionals	
Step ①:	Assign paraprofessionals to classrooms, grade levels, groups of students, or even an entire building as floaters to support students and educators as needed.
Step ②:	For students assigned a 1:1 paraprofessional, determine if the 1:1 support is still necessary in a new inclusive system.

Source: From *The Inclusive System Scheduling Process* by J. Causton, K. MacLeod, & K. Pretti-Frontczak, 2022, Inclusive Schooling.

Appendix F: Co-Teaching Models

Co-Teaching Model	Description
More Effective, Use Frequently ***These models reduce student-to-teacher ratios and increase opportunities for staff responsiveness, differentiation, and staff parity.***	
Station	Teachers divide instructional content into two, three, or more segments and present it in separate locations within the classroom or throughout the school. Stations are sometimes called *centers*.
One-teach/ one-make multisensory	One teacher leads the lesson/activity and the other teacher increases the number of access points by adding more tools, examples, visuals, and strategies simultaneously.
Parallel	The class is split into two sections, with each teacher delivering content to a smaller group, often using different teaching approaches and strategies. For example, one teacher shows how to add numbers and objects using manipulatives and the other teacher shows how to add through drawing picture stories. Often the groups of students then switch so all students learn from both teachers and both approaches.
Less Effective, Use Strategically ***These models do not reduce student-to-teacher ratios or significantly increase either differentiation opportunities or staff parity.***	
Duet	Both teachers engage in primary teaching roles with the whole class at the same time. Teachers collaboratively provide content, lead class discussions, answer questions, facilitate activities, and assess learning.
One-teach/ one-assist	One teacher leads the lesson and the other teacher circulates through the room providing seamless and embedded support to specific students as needed. The one assisting might help differentiate on the spot by clarifying something, extending an idea, or providing an example.
One-teach/ one-float	One teacher leads the lesson while the other teacher supports the whole class in some way. The teacher who is floating often prepares materials, sets up the next activity with needed modifications, distributes supplies, or collects data.

Source: From *Co-Teaching Models* by J. Causton & K. Pretti-Frontczak, 2021, Inclusive Schooling. Copyright 2021 by Inclusive Schooling. Reprinted with permission.

Appendix G: Inclusive Classroom Practices Resources

Collaboration and Co-Teaching

- **Article:** Hackett, J., Kruzich, J., Goulter, A., & Battista, M. (2021). Tearing down the invisible walls: Designing, implementing, and theorizing psychologically safer co-teaching for inclusion. *Journal of Educational Change, 22*(1), 103–130.
- **Article:** Pancsofar, N., & Petroff, J. G. (2013). Professional development experiences in co-teaching: Associations with teacher confidence, interests, and attitudes. *Teacher Education and Special Education, 36*(2), 83–96.
- **Book:** Kluth, P., & Causton, J. (2016). *30 days to the co-taught classroom: How to curate an amazing, nearly miraculous & practically earth-shattering partnership in one month or less.* CreateSpace.
- **Online Course:** *Co-teaching for the inclusive classroom: Creating phenomenal co-teaching teams* [Online course]. (2021). Inclusive Schooling. www.inclusiveschooling.com/product/co-teaching-for-inclusive-classrooms-on-demand-series/

Differentiation

- **Article:** Bondie, R. S., Dahnke, C., & Zusho, A. (2019). How does changing "one-size-fits-all" to differentiated instruction affect teaching? *Review of Research in Education, 43*(1), 336–362.
- **Article:** Lindner, K. T., & Schwab, S. (2020). Differentiation and individualisation in inclusive education: A systematic review and narrative synthesis. *International Journal of Inclusive Education*, 1–21.
- **Book:** Tomlinson, C. A. (2017). *How to differentiate instruction in academically diverse classrooms*. ASCD.
- **Online Course:** *Differentiated instruction made practical.* https://pll.harvard.edu/course/differentiated-instruction-made-practical

Creating Adaptations

- **Article:** Causton, J., Udvari-Solner, A., & MacLeod, K. M. (2017). Creating educational adaptations, accommodations, and modifications. In F. P. Orelove, D. Sobsey, & D. L. Gilles (Eds.), *Educating students with severe and multiple disabilities: A collaborative approach* (5th ed., pp. 407–435). Brookes.
- **Book:** Kurth, J. A., & Gross, M. N. (2014). *The inclusion toolbox: Strategies and techniques for all teachers*. Corwin.

Providing Natural Supports

- **Article:** Causton-Theoharis, J. N. (2009). The golden rule of providing support in inclusive classrooms: Support others as you would wish to be supported. *Teaching Exceptional Children, 42*(2), 36–43. www.inclusion-ny.org/files/GoldenRule-1.pdf
- **Article:** Carter, E. W., Sisco, L. G., Melekoglu, M. A., & Kurkowski, C. (2007). Peer supports as an alternative to individually assigned paraprofessionals in inclusive high school classrooms. *Research and Practice for Persons with Severe Disabilities, 32*(4), 213–227.
- **Book:** Carter, E., Cushing, L., & Kennedy, C. (2008). *Peer support strategies for improving all students' social lives and learning*. Brookes.
- **Book:** Causton, J., & MacLeod, K. (2020). *The paraprofessional's handbook for effective support in inclusive classrooms* (2nd ed.). Brookes.

Providing Behavior Supports

- **Article:** Causton, J., MacLeod, K., & Pretti-Frontczak, K. (2021). Ready... set... success: A formula for leading schools with love. *Educational Leadership, 79*(2), 21–25. www.ascd.org/el/articles/ready-set-success-a-formula-for-leading-schools-with-love

- **Book:** Causton, J., & MacLeod, K. (2020). *From behaving to belonging: The inclusive art of supporting students who challenge us*. ASCD.
- **Online Course:** *Beyond treats and timeouts: Support for challenging behaviors on-demand.* www.inclusiveschooling.com/product/2021-beyond-treats-and-timeouts-support-for-challenging-behaviors-on-demand/

Inclusive Classroom Practices

- **Article:** Finkelstein, S., Sharma, U., & Furlonger, B. (2021). The inclusive practices of classroom teachers: A scoping review and thematic analysis. *International Journal of Inclusive Education, 25*(6), 735–762.
- **Book:** Woodlock, M., & Novak, K. (2021). *UDL Playbook for School and District Leaders*. Cast.
- **Online Modules:** The Iris Center Peabody College. (2021). *High-Leverage Practices*. Vanderbilt University. https://iris.peabody.vanderbilt.edu/resources/high-leverage-practices/
- **Report:** Jorgensen, C. M., McSheehan, M., Schuh, M., & Sonnenmeier, R. M. (2012, July). *Essential best practices in inclusive schools*. National Center on Inclusive Education, Institute on Disability / UCED, University of New Hampshire.

References

Berger, J. (2020). *The catalyst: How to change anyone's mind.* Simon & Schuster.

Bouillet, D. (2013). Some aspects of collaboration in inclusive education: Teachers' experiences. *Center for Educational Policy Studies Journal, 3*(2), 93–117.

Brock, M. E., Biggs, E. E., Carter, E. W., Cattey, G. N., & Raley, K. S. (2016). Implementation and generalization of peer support arrangements for students with severe disabilities in inclusive classrooms. *The Journal of Special Education, 49*(4), 221–232.

Brown v. Board of Education of Topeka, 347 U.S. 483 (1954).

Cameron, D. L. (2014). An examination of teacher–student interactions in inclusive classrooms: Teacher interviews and classroom observations. *Journal of Research in Special Educational Needs, 14*(4), 264–273.

Causton, J., & MacLeod, K. (2022a). *Equity review data collection guide.* Inclusive Schooling.

Causton, J., & MacLeod, K. (2022b). *Inclusive classroom observation tool.* Inclusive Schooling.

Causton, J., & MacLeod, K. (2022c). *Inclusive system focus group survey.* Inclusive Schooling.

Causton, J., & MacLeod, K. (2022d). *Inclusive reform service-delivery map examples.* Inclusive Schooling.

Causton, J., MacLeod, K., & Pretti-Frontczak, K. (2022a). *The inclusive system change path.* Inclusive Schooling.

Causton, J., MacLeod, K., & Pretti-Frontczak, K. (2022b). *The inclusive system scheduling process.* Inclusive Schooling.

Causton, J., MacLeod, K., & Pretti-Frontczak, K. (2022c). *Collaborative and inclusive service delivery.* Inclusive Schooling.

Causton, J., & Pretti-Frontczak, K. (2021a). *Inclusive education: A re-imagined definition of inclusion.* Inclusive Schooling.

Causton, J., & Pretti-Frontczak, K. (2021b). *The transition from medical to equity lens.* Inclusive Schooling.

Causton, J., & Pretti-Frontczak, K. (2021c). *The four Ss of leadership.* Inclusive Schooling.

Causton, J., & Pretti-Frontczak, K. (2021d). *Co-teaching models.* Inclusive Schooling.

Causton-Theoharis, J. N., & Malmgren, K. W. (2005). Increasing peer interactions for students with severe disabilities via paraprofessional training. *Exceptional Children, 71*(4), 431–444.

Choi, J. H., McCart, A. B., & Sailor, W. (2020). Achievement of students with IEPs and associated relationships with an inclusive MTSS framework. *The Journal of Special Education, 54*(3).

Choi, J. H., Meisenheimer, J. M., McCart, A. B., & Sailor, W. (2017). Improving learning for all students through equity-based inclusive reform practices: Effectiveness of a fully integrated schoolwide model on student reading and math achievement. *Remedial and Special Education, 38*(1), 28–41.

Cole, C. M., Waldron, N., & Majd, M. (2004). Academic progress of students across inclusive and traditional settings. *Mental Retardation, 42*(2), 136–144.

Copeland, S. R., & Cosbey, J. (2009). Making progress in the general education curriculum: Rethinking effective instructional practices. *Research and Practice for Persons with Severe Disabilities, 33*(4), 214–227.

Cordingley, P., Higgins, S., Greany, T., Buckler, N., Coles-Jordan, D., Crisp, B., et al. (2015). *Developing great teaching: Lessons from the international reviews into effective professional development* [Project report]. Teacher Development Trust.

Cosier, M., Causton-Theoharis, J., & Theoharis, G. (2013). Does access matter? Time in general education and achievement for students with disabilities. *Remedial and Special Education, 34*(6), 323–332.

Daniel R. R. v. State Board of Education, 874 F.2d 1036 (5th Cir. 1989).

Dessemontet, R. S., Bless, G., & Morin, D. (2011). Effect of inclusion on the academic achievement and adaptive behaviour of children with intellectual disabilities. *Journal of Intellectual Disability Research, 56*(6), 579–587.

DeVita, M. C., Colvin, R. L., Darling-Hammond, L., & Haycock, K. (2007). *Education leadership: A bridge to school reform*. The Wallace Foundation's National Conference. The Wallace Foundation.

DuFour, R., & Eaker, R. (2009). *Revisiting professional learning communities at work*. Hawker Brownlow Education.

Endrew F. v. Douglas County School District Re-1, 137 U.S. 988. (2017).

Fink, L. D. (2013). *Creating significant learning experiences: An integrated approach to designing college courses*. John Wiley & Sons.

Fisher, D., Frey, N., & Thousand, J. (2003). What do special educators need to know and be prepared to do for inclusive schooling to work? *Teacher Education and Special Education, 26*(1), 42–50.

Foreman, P., Arthur-Kelly, M., Pascoe, S., & Smyth King, B. (2004). Evaluating the educational experiences of students with profound and multiple disabilities in inclusive and segregated classroom settings: An Australian perspective. *Research and Practice for Persons with Severe Disabilities, 29*(3), 183–193.

Giangreco, M. F., Suter, J. C., & Doyle, M. B. (2010). Paraprofessionals in inclusive schools: A review of recent research. *Journal of Educational and Psychological Consultation, 20*(1), 41–57.

Hackett, J., Kruzich, J., Goulter, A., & Battista, M. (2021). Tearing down the invisible walls: Designing, implementing, and theorizing psychologically safer co-teaching for inclusion. *Journal of Educational Change, 22*(1), 103–130.

Hehir, T., Grindal, T., Freeman, B., Lamoreau, R., Borquaye, Y., & Burke, S. (2016, August). *A summary of the evidence on inclusive education*. Available from Abt Associates, 4550 Montgomery Ave., Ste. 800 N., Bethesda, MD 20814.

Hehir, T., & Katzman, L. I. (2012). *Effective inclusive schools: Designing successful schoolwide programs*. Jossey-Bass.

Hunter, W., Jasper, A. D., & Williamson, R. L. (2014). Utilizing middle school common planning time to support inclusive environments. *Intervention in School and Clinic, 50*(2), 114–120.

Individuals with Disabilities Education Act, 20 USC § 1400 (2004).

Jackson, L. B., Ryndak, D. L., & Wehmeyer, M. L. (2008). The dynamic relationship between context, curriculum, and student learning: A case for inclusive education as a research-based practice. *Research and Practice for Persons with Severe Disabilities, 34*(1), 175–195.

Krajewski, J., & Hyde, M. S. (2000). Comparison of teen attitudes toward individuals with mental retardation between 1987 and 1998: Has inclusion made a difference? *Education and Training in Mental Retardation and Developmental Disabilities, 35*(3), 284–293.

Kuntz, E. M., & Carter, E. W. (2021). General educators' involvement in interventions for students with intellectual disability. *Inclusion, 9*(2), 134–150.

Kurth, J. A., & Keegan, L. (2014). Development and use of curricular adaptations for students receiving special education services. *The Journal of Special Education, 48*(3), 191–203.

Kurth, J., & Mastergeorge, A. M. (2010). Individual education plan goals and services for adolescents with autism: Impact of age and educational setting. *The Journal of Special Education, 44*(3), 146–160.

Lee, S. H., Wehmeyer, M. L., Soukup, J. H., & Palmer, S. B. (2010). Impact of curriculum modifications on access to the general education curriculum for students with disabilities. *Exceptional Children, 76*(2), 213–233.

L. H. v. Hamilton County Department of Education, No. 18-5086 (6th Cir. 2018).

Mazzotti, V. L., Rowe, D. A., Kwiatek, S., Voggt, A., Chang, W. H., Fowler, C. H., et al. (2021). Secondary transition predictors of postschool success: An update to the research base. *Career Development and Transition for Exceptional Individuals, 44*(1), 47–64.

McCart, A., & Miller, D. (2019). *Leading equity-based MTSS for all students.* Corwin.

McDuffie, K. A., Mastropieri, M. A., & Scruggs, T. (2009). Differential effects of peer tutoring in co-taught and non-co-taught classes: Results for content learning and student-teacher interactions. *Exceptional Children, 75,* 493–510.

McManus, G. (2013, September). A speedy road to skill acquisition. *Management Today,* 18–19.

National Center for Education Statistics. (2022). *Fast facts: Students with disabilities, the inclusion of.* United States Department of Education. https://nces.ed.gov/fastfacts/display.asp?id=59

National Longitudinal Transition Study. (1993). Institute of Education Sciences, U.S. Department of Education.

National Longitudinal Transition Study-2. (2004). *Facts from NLTS2: School behavior and disciplinary experiences of youth with disabilities.* Institute of Education Sciences, U.S. Department of Education.

National Longitudinal Transition Study-2. (2006). *Facts from NLTS2: School behavior and disciplinary experiences of youth with disabilities (March 2006).* Menlo Park, CA: SRI International. www.nlts2.org/fact_sheets/nlts2_fact_sheet_2006_03.pdf

National Longitudinal Transition Study-2012. (2012). Institute of Education Sciences, U.S. Department of Education.

Newman, L., Wagner, M., Cameto, R., Knokey, A. M., & Shaver, D. (2010). *Comparisons across time of the outcomes of youth with disabilities up to four years after high school: A report of findings from the National Longitudinal Transition Study (NLTS) and the National Longitudinal Transition Study-2 (NLTS2).* National Center for Special Education Research. (NCSER 2010-3008)

Oberti v. Board of Education of Clementon School District, 801 F. Supp. 1392 (DNJ 1992).

Pennsylvania Association for Retarded Citizens (PARC) v. Commonwealth of Pennsylvania, 334 F. Supp. 1257 (ED Pa. 1972).

Roncker v. Walter, 700 F.2d 1058 (6th Cir. 1983).

Rufo, J. M., & Causton, J. (2022). *Reimagining special education: Using inclusion as a framework to build equity and support all students.* Brookes.

Sacramento City Unified School District v. Rachel H., 14 F.3d 1398 (9th Cir. 1994).

Salerno, A., & Brock, L. (2022). *The Change Cycle.* Change Cycle. https://changecycle.com/change-cycle

Scruggs, T., Mastropieri, M. A., & McDuffie, K. A. (2007). Co-teaching in inclusive classrooms: A meta-synthesis of qualitative research. *Exceptional Children, 73,* 392–416.

Sheridan, S. M., Edwards, C. P., Marvin, C. A., & Knoche, L. L. (2009). Professional development in early childhood programs: Process issues and research needs. *Early Education and Development, 20*(3), 377–401.

Shogren, K. A., Gross, J. M., Forber-Pratt, A. J., Francis, G. L., Satter, A. L., Blue-Banning, M., et al. (2015). The perspectives of students with and without disabilities on inclusive schools. *Research and Practice for Persons with Severe Disabilities, 40*(4), 243–260.

Siegel, D. J., & Bryson, T. P. (2020). *The power of showing up: How parental presence shapes who our kids become and how their brains get wired.* Ballantine Books.

Skiba, R. J., & Losen, D. J. (2016). From reaction to prevention: Turning the page on school discipline. *American Educator, 39*(4), 4.

Taylor, S. (2017). *Contested knowledge: A critical review of the concept of differentiation in teaching and learning*. School of Education, Worcester University.

Test, D. W., Mazzotti, V. L., Mustian, A. L., Fowler, C. H., Kortering, L., & Kohler, P. (2009). Evidence-based secondary transition predictors for improving postschool outcomes for students with disabilities. *Career Development for Exceptional Individuals, 32*(3), 160–181.

U.S. Department of Education, National Center for Education Statistics. (2021). *Digest of Education Statistics, 2019*. U.S. Department of Education. (NCES 2021-009).

U.S. Department of Education. (2020). OSEP fast facts: Children identified with emotional disturbance. *IDEA*. https://sites.ed.gov/idea/osep-fast-facts-children-IDed-Emotional-Disturbance-20

Wagner, M., Newman, L., Cameto, R., & Levine, P. (2006). *The academic performance and functional achievement of youth with disabilities*. SRI International.

Woodman, A. C., Smith, L. E., Greenberg, J. S., & Mailick, M. R. (2016). Contextual factors predict patterns of change in functioning over 10 years among adolescents and adults with autism spectrum disorders. *Journal of Autism and Developmental Disorders, 46*(1), 176–189.

Index

The letter *f* following a page number denotes a figure.

About the Authors

Dr. Julie Causton is a best-selling author, inspiring speaker, and inclusive education advocate. The founder and CEO of Inclusive Schooling, she is a former tenured professor in the Inclusive and Special Education Program in the Department of Teaching and Leadership at Syracuse University, where she headed the Inclusive Elementary Education Program. Julie has spent the last 25 years studying best practices for inclusive education. A former elementary, middle, and high school special education teacher herself, she knows firsthand how inclusion leads to better outcomes for students. With Dr. Kristie Pretti-Frontczak, she has conducted magical presentations focusing on engaging ways to educate all students within the context of general education that have inspired and uplifted administrators, teachers, paraprofessionals, and families throughout the United States and helped them learn the most cutting-edge inclusive practices. Julie is the author of a dozen books about inclusive education, and she has published articles in over 30 educational research and practitioner journals. She currently resides in upstate New York.

Dr. Kate MacLeod is an innovative inclusive educator, researcher, and author. She began her career as a high school special education teacher in New York City and now works as faculty in the college of education at the University of Maine Farmington and as an education consultant with Inclusive Schooling. She has spent 15 years studying inclusive practices and supporting school leaders and educators to feel prepared and inspired to include all learners. She lives in Maine with her husband and son.

Dr. Kristie Pretti-Frontczak is a highly sought-after speaker, accomplished author, and educators' educator. With nearly three decades of educational experience, including 16 years as faculty at Kent State University, Kristie cultivates real change within educational systems. She instills an impressive sense of joy, humor, and fun in creating inclusive educational practices and empowering teachers and leaders to spread wellness both within and beyond the classroom walls. At Inclusive Schooling, along with Dr. Julie Causton, Kristie designs and delivers transformative professional development that addresses and supports the wholeness of the adult professional and helps leaders create school cultures that ensure all children experience a sense of belonging. She has published extensively in peer-reviewed journals and is an author of over 10 books and monographs. Since 2013, she has followed her true passion, which is supporting adult learners. As a result, she has accumulated over 50,000 hours of helping educators and leaders work from a place of compassion, hope, and love in locations from Cincinnati to Singapore. She currently resides in northeastern Ohio.

Dr. Jenna Mancini Rufo is an experienced public-school leader turned inclusive education consultant. She is the founder and owner of empowerED School Solutions, a consulting firm specializing in equity and inclusion. Having served as an assistant superintendent, director of special education, state policy specialist, special education teacher, and inclusion facilitator, Jenna has practical experience in leading systems change for inclusion. She has shared her knowledge at numerous events, including *The Atlantic*'s Education Summit and the National Principals' Conference. She has been published in *School Administrator* and recently launched a blog and video series. Jenna was inspired to enter the field of education by her sister, Nina, who has multiple disabilities. She views education as her calling and is passionate about providing quality programs for *all* students.

Dr. Paul Gordon is an educator who has dedicated his life to public education. Paul spent much of his career working for the Adams 12 Five Star School District outside Denver, Colorado, where he served as a classroom teacher, a middle school principal, the director of professional development, and the chief academic officer. During the last 10 years, Paul has served as the superintendent of three school districts. Early in Paul's career, he worked with students with significant reading challenges, which forged his path toward creating inclusive environments for each student. The districts Paul has worked with have engaged in honest conversations about inclusive practices and the incredible opportunities and challenges that districts and schools must understand as they embrace this important work for students. He has worked with educators in Colorado, Illinois, and Washington who have influenced his beliefs about students, instruction, systems, and families. As a working practitioner, Paul profoundly understands the complexity of what it means to create inclusive environments for students and the impact it has on the overall system. He continues to learn from students, teachers, directors, parents, and countless others working in our inclusive classrooms daily about the challenges and the incredible opportunities that inclusion offers each student.

Related ASCD Resources: Inclusive Education

At the time of publication, the following resources were available (ASCD stock numbers appear in parentheses).

Brain-Friendly Strategies for the Inclusion Classroom by Judy Willis (#107040E4)

Building on the Strengths of Students with Special Needs: How to Move Beyond Disability Labels in the Classroom by Toby J. Karten (#117023)

Creating an Inclusive School, 2nd Edition by Richard A. Villa and Jacqueline S. Thousand (Eds.) (#105019E4)

Decoding Autism and Leading the Way to Successful Inclusion by Barbara Boroson (#118008)

From Behaving to Belonging: The Inclusive Art of Supporting Students Who Challenge Us by Julie Causton and Kate MacLeod (#121011)

From Goals to Growth: Intervention and Support in Every Classroom by Lee Ann Jung (#118032)

Inclusion Do's, Don'ts, and Do Betters (Quick Reference Guide) by Toby J. Karten (#QRG116082)

Leading an Inclusive School: Access and Success for ALL Students by Richard A. Villa and Jacqueline S. Thousand (#116022)

A Teacher's Guide to Special Education by David F. Bateman and Jenifer L. Cline (#116019)

Teaching in Tandem: Effective Co-Teaching in the Inclusive Classroom by Gloria Lodato Wilson and Joan Blednick (#110029)

Trauma-Informed Teaching and IEPs: Strategies for Building Student Resilience by Melissa Sadin (#122026)

Your Students, My Students, Our Students: Rethinking Equitable and Inclusive Classrooms by Lee Ann Jung, Nancy Frey, Douglas Fisher, and Julie Kroener (#119019)

For up-to-date information about ASCD resources, go to **www.ascd.org.** You can search the complete archives of *Educational Leadership* at **www.ascd.org /el.**

ASCD myTeachSource®

Download resources from a professional learning platform with hundreds of research-based best practices and tools for your classroom at http://myteach source.ascd.org/.

For more information, send an email to member@ascd.org; call 1-800-933-2723 or 703-578-9600; send a fax to 703-575-5400; or write to Information Services, ASCD, 2800 Shirlington Road, Suite 1001, Arlington, VA 22206 USA.